Noble Character

Becoming a Daughter of
Victory & Virtue

Tiffany M. Schlichter

Noble Girlhood: Becoming a Daughter of Victory and Virtue

Copyright © 2006 by Tiffany M. Schlichter.
All Rights Reserved.
Printed in the United States of America.

While this book is protected by copyright, the author welcomes the copying of an occasional page for the encouragement of others, provided the source and ordering information is given. Thank you.

Scriptures taken from the King James Version (KJV) of the Holy Bible.

Published by *Virtuous Daughters*
Edited by Mrs. Cheryl L. Schlichter
Cover design and typography by Tiffany M. Schlichter

ISBN # 1-59872-418-5

Other books by this author: *Encouragement to the Home School Student*, 2003

To my dear sisters in **Virtuous Daughters**—*never grow weary in striving to be the daughters you are called to be.*

To my precious sister, Brittany— continue seeking Jesus' face!

And especially to my dear mother—for all the time she has invested in teaching me to love and serve the King.

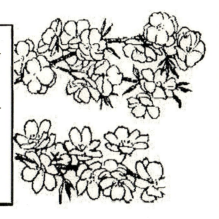

CONTENTS

Dear Sister 9
How to Use this Book 11
Preface 13

1. Becoming a Daughter of Victory 15
      The Good Shepherd 26

2. Becoming a Daughter of Devotion 29
      The Life of Prayer 42

3. Becoming a Daughter of Purpose 45
      God's Design for Ministry 59

4. Becoming a Daughter of Delight 63
      The Best Gift You Can Ever Give Your Parents 77

5. Becoming a Sister of Love 83
      Making Your Brother Your Best Friend 96

6. Becoming a Daughter of Discernment 101
      Bless Your Pen Pal 114

7. Becoming a Daughter of Honor 117
      Maxims for Health & Gracefulness 131

8. Becoming a Daughter of Wisdom 135
      The Dog Puppy 146

9. Becoming a Daughter of Beauty 149
      A Wordless Indicator 165

10. Becoming a Daughter of Purity 167
        Discernment in Reading 177

11. Becoming a Daughter of the Home 183
        Scheduling Tips.. 198

12. Becoming a Daughter of Service 201

Give Her the Fruit of Her Hands 217
Peter Marshall's Challenge to American Women 218
Godly Resources 219
Bibliography 220
With Gratitude 223
Also Available Through Virtuous Daughters 224
Order Form 225
Mail-In Form 226
Notes 227
About the Author 228
The Story Behind this Book 229

Dear Sister,

Praise the Lord that there are other young women who long to be virtuous! What a noble goal! Sometimes this goal seems far-fetched; it entails strength and courage. Let me encourage you to take the precious guidance of the Lord Jesus in all you do—He will help you every step of the way. Read His Word and seek His wisdom as you lead a life that glorifies and honors Him.

Who am I? Why am I here? Will God ever be able to use my life for any profitable reason, or will I spend it aimlessly, never exercising my full potential? These are questions every girl faces, and the world offers foolish suggestions. It is my prayer that in this book you are encouraged to draw from Scriptures the answers to these mysteries.

My name is Tiffany Schlichter. I am sixteen years old and nearing the end of tenth grade. I am home educated by my wonderful parents, Dan and Cheryl, and am the eldest of five children—Justin (thirteen), Brittany (nine), Gideon (five), and Ethan (two). Our family lives on five wooded acres in Montgomery, Texas. We enjoy the outdoors and spending time together.

My main goal in life is to bring glory and honor to my Lord and Savior, Jesus Christ. I hope that He uses the words He has so graciously given in this book to encourage you to press on in well doing! Do not grow weary; you will reap if you faint not! (See Galatians 6:9.)

Think of your life as a pilgrimage—the end will be glorious when you come face to face with your Savior. As you journey, keep your life focused on the Lord, for Whom you are running this race. Continue in what He has called you to do! "I press toward the mark for the prize of the high calling of God in Christ Jesus." —Philippians 3:14

Because I realize you are taking time and effort to read this book, I would like to offer a small token of appreciation if you complete it cover to cover (that includes the applications!☺). When you are finished, simply fill out the form in the back and mail it to me. Lastly, please do not read this book if you have not sought the Lord today through prayer and reading of His Word. What I have to offer is nothing compared to the priceless jewels and treasures found in the Holy Bible.

Also, please understand as you read this book that God is working with me on every topic I write about! Quite often, I get off the computer and think, "Oh, I could improve so much in this area." As one author put it, "my finger points back at me as I write." However, by writing what the Lord is teaching me, it pressures me to dwell on those lessons more, and I have an easier time applying them.☺ Just remember that we are running this race together!

May the Lord bless you as you continually seek His face, and may you grow in the grace and knowledge of our Lord Jesus Christ!

Because He Lives,

Tiffany♡

"For I know the thoughts that I think toward you, saith the LORD, thoughts of peace, and not of evil, to give you an expected end. Then shall ye call upon me, and ye shall go and pray unto me, and I will hearken unto you. And ye shall seek me, and find me, when ye shall search for me with all your heart."—Jeremiah 29:11–13

How To Use This Book...

This is your book, and you can use it however you wish! ☺ *However, let me explain the layout so you can better understand the intended way to use it.*

♥ First is each chapter. Keep a Bible handy, and, like a good Berean Christian, take what I have said and compare it to God's Word. Look up for yourself the Scriptures provided. Please remember that this book is simply a compilation of thoughts and insights—things that I have learned. By no means is it infallible truth, nor does it replace reading from God's Word. The Bible is the only absolute truth and the only thing you need as a Christian to understand how to live this life. What I have to say, prayerfully, will simply point you back to Jesus Christ. So before reading each chapter, read from the Bible. What the Lord has to say to you in His Word is far more important and instructional than anything I could ever write. (Not only because God inspired it, but also because the Holy Spirit will reveal Jesus Christ to you through the Word.)

♥ Second is the suggested resources. These are some "tools" I have appreciated and been encouraged by. They provide more wisdom and instruction on the topic discussed.

♥ Third is an extra thought. These are articles that have been printed in the *Virtuous Daughters* magazine, and may be of encouragement on the particular topic discussed.

♥ Fourth is the application. Each of these will have questions and activities to help apply and reinforce the truths in each chapter.

᛫ *What is Virtuous Daughters? Virtuous Daughters*, as you will find by reading the book, is a small magazine that I publish on a monthly basis. The goal of it is to encourage young ladies to grow in the Lord Jesus Christ. It started when I was twelve years old, and the Lord has been blessing it ever since. For information about subscribing, simply write to me.

Blessings—*Tiffany*

Preface...
"Virtuous Daughters"
By Mrs. Cheryl Schlichter

Darling virtuous daughters,
This you long to be.
And such a noble goal,
For you will one day see.

By allowing God to mold you,
To conform you with His hands;
You become a priceless jewel,
The rarest of the lands.

So do you see dear darlings?
The work in you has begun.
By living today as a virtuous daughter,
A virtuous woman you become.

"Who can find a virtuous woman? for her price is far above rubies."—Proverbs 31:10

–Chapter 1–
Becoming a Daughter of Victory

"But thanks be to God, which giveth us the victory through our Lord Jesus Christ. Therefore, my beloved brethren, be ye stedfast, unmoveable, always abounding in the work of the Lord, forasmuch as ye know that your labour is not in vain in the Lord."
—1 Corinthians 15:57–58

Achieving Victory Over Sin and Self
In the Christian Pilgrimage

Lisa sighed, "So often I feel defeated. There's just too much that I need to work on—too much sin to conquer."

"I know how you feel," Beth looked at her friend. "What we need is victory, but I don't know how to achieve it. We want to be good—you know—virtuous and all, but, well, I just don't think I can."

What Lisa and Beth are lacking is victory. The only way to acquire it is through Jesus Christ—Jesus is the Victor!

We Fall Short

Many young women lack victory in their Christian lives. They are unsure how to attain it. The thought of becoming a virtuous daughter can be overwhelming.

I read the Proverbs 31 passage. Discouraging thoughts filled my heart. "There's no way. This is literally impossible." I felt that I could never succeed as a virtuous daughter. There is so much sin to conquer, so much to become that I am not! I knew that in myself, I could never reach my destined goal.

I was right. We cannot be good in our own selves. We can never be daughters of virtue in our flesh. The truth is that in self, we are all sinners and fall sadly short of the glory of God. *"For all have sinned and come short of the glory of God."—Romans 3:23*

Every Christian has three main enemies. They are 1) Satan 2) The World 3) The Flesh. Which do you think is our greatest enemy? While many would say Satan, it is actually our very own flesh. How awful and ugly that flesh is! It constantly seems to be in the way of what we know is right.

Christ Gives the Victory

"I am the vine, ye are the branches: he that abideth in Me, and I in him, the same bringeth forth much fruit: for without Me ye can do nothing."—John 15:5

Despite the first unpromising facts, joyous news of hope and victory lie on the horizon . . . God's Word promises us that *through Christ* we can have victory over our *sins* and *ourselves*. When Christ was crucified on the cross, so was SELF. Every day, we must continue to die to self, and allow the Lord to do His precious work in our lives.

When Christ is working through us, we are allowing His righteousness to flow through us, and therefore we are fit to do things that honor and glorify Him. What reassuring news! Do not be deceived, however; we must never forget that victory is *only* through Christ Jesus. As one pastor put it, "We must come to this humbling point in life: that God cannot use us until there is nothing of us, and all of Him."

I appreciate the following excerpt from the book, *Abide in Christ*, by Mr. Forrest Wychopen:

"So with determination we have purposed to live the Christian life. With the discipline of militant soldiers we have purposed to follow Jesus. I will live a Godly life. I will pray without ceasing. I will study to show myself approved unto God. I will attend church regularly. I will tell at least one person every day about Jesus Christ . . . I will obey my parents . . . I will work heartily as unto the Lord and not unto men. And on and on and on. We quote the Apostle Paul and declare, 'I will fight a good fight, I will keep the faith, and I will finish the course.'

"Do not misunderstand me, I agree that God calls us to obey Him and do all that He commands us to do. That is the entire point of John 15:5. You can do nothing without Him! Yes, God desires for us to do something—to be active in His affairs. God desires for us to walk in truth. But the point remains the same, nothing happens without Jesus Christ. Good works that are not produced from abiding in Christ are nothing more than works of the flesh. The key to a fruitful, productive, joyful, and abounding life is Jesus Christ—the True Vine! Let it sink in Believer, without Him, we can do nothing.

". . . One of the hardest things for us to do in the Christian life is to let go of our will and allow Christ to live His life through us. The idea that we must do our part in order to live the Christian life is so firmly

grounded in our way of thinking that surrender is the last thing on our mind. But surrender is exactly what you and I must do! Abide in Christ, for without Him you can do nothing, but through Christ, you can do all things!"

The Race for Victory

"Wherefore seeing we also are compassed about with so great a cloud of witnesses, let us lay aside every weight, and the sin which doth so easily beset us, and let us run with patience the race that is set before us, looking unto Jesus the author and finisher of our faith; who for the joy that was set before Him endured the cross, despising the shame, and is set down at the right hand of the throne of God. For consider Him that endured such contradiction of sinners against Himself, lest ye be wearied and faint in your minds."—Hebrews 12:1–3

When someone enters a racing competition, he does not carry a backpack, nor does he wear heavy shoes. These would only reduce the rate at which he could run. Keeping his goal in sight, he brings as little gear as possible but also the necessary gear to complete the race.

The above verses remind us that in the race we are to run as Christians, to put aside all worries, fears, or burdens, which could get in the way. Then we are instructed to rid ourselves of sin. Living the Christian life in sin will weigh us down. It is not a life of virtue.

Lastly, we are to run with patience, only looking to Jesus, because in this race, He is all that matters. He is the goal. He is the focus. He is the victory. *"Let thine eyes look right on, and let thine eyelids look straight before thee. Ponder the path of thy feet, and let all thy ways be established. Turn not to the right hand nor to the left: remove thy foot from evil."—Proverbs 4:25–27*

We stray by sinning, which makes getting "back on track" difficult. We long to be running the glorious race again, but the burden of sin is a challenge.

Thankfully, our God is a merciful God. When we slip to the side because we were not looking straight ahead, He comes over as the Good Shepherd and places us back in the direction to victory in Jesus. When we ask for forgiveness, He lovingly grants this request.

"Who is a God like unto thee, that pardoneth iniquity, and passeth by the

transgression of the remnant of his heritage? He retaineth not his anger for ever, because He delighteth in mercy. He will turn again, He will have compassion upon us; He will subdue our iniquities; and thou wilt cast all their sins into the depths of the sea."—Micah 7:18–19

"The LORD is merciful and gracious, slow to anger, and plenteous in mercy . . . He hath not dealt with us after our sins; nor rewarded us according to our iniquities. For as the heaven is high above the earth, so great is His mercy toward them that fear Him. As far as the east is from the west, so far hath He removed our transgressions from us. Like as a father pitieth His children, so the LORD pitieth them that fear him."—Psalm 103:8, 10–13

"God [wants us to learn] patience and endurance. After I make a mistake, my first impulse is to throw everything away and march off vowing to never cook again; but this is not what God would have me to do. He wants me to go back, and show endurance and patience, [and] stick with it. Not only in cooking am I faced with these challenges, but with many other aspects of life such as sewing, cleaning my room, and walking with the Lord. A lot of times after I have hurt someone or showed disrespect to my parents I feel terrible, but don't want to go back and ask forgiveness. However, Jesus tells me to have endurance and repair my relationship by asking forgiveness. I have learned that everything, even little things like cooking failures, are used by Christ to teach me to conform more to His image and trust His leading, and I pray that I never ignore His promptings—don't you?"

—Brianna Auge, in *Virtuous Daughters*

Praise the Lord for His loving mercy and kindness. Rejoice in the truth that there is hope in Jesus Christ—our Lord and Savior—for all who believe in Him and have yielded their lives to Him! Press on in what He is calling you to do!

One Big Hindrance

"Holding faith, and a good conscience; which some having put away concerning faith have made shipwreck."—1 Timothy 1:19

One of the biggest hindrances in the Christian walk is a guilty conscience. I have had to deal with a guilty conscience before, and it was definitely a burden in my race! To continue running with joy and victory, we *must* lay aside this weight. *"He that covereth his sins shall not prosper: but whoso confesseth and forsaketh them shall have mercy."*—Proverbs 28:13

How, then, do we lay aside this weight? We must sincerely ask the Lord's forgiveness for sins that we have not confessed. *"If we confess our sins, He is faithful and just to forgive us our sins, and to cleanse us from all unrighteousness."*—1 John 1:9 If the sin offended someone else, we must go to that person and ask his forgiveness as well. Of course it does not stop here. We must *forsake* our sins. We must stop doing them!

This is not an easy process to go through, but the results are wonderful! I had to clear my conscience of several things when I was about eleven or twelve years old, and it was one of the best decisions I made as a Christian. It strengthened my walk with my family and my walk with the Lord. *"Having a good conscience; that, whereas they speak evil of you, as of evildoers, they may be ashamed that falsely accuse your good conversation in Christ."*—1 Peter 3:16

Once the Lord and those we have offended have forgiven us, we must forgive *ourselves*. Our pastor preached an excellent sermon on this at the beginning of a new year, and I was very encouraged! I was reminded that there is no reason to go through life upset with myself for things I have done, when God has already forgiven me! I have to lay those things aside, and continue with the Christian walk. They are still there, and I must accept them. There are still consequences of sin, but I do not have to let them hinder my walk by allowing doubt and guilt to discourage me. If we are forgiven, we cannot let our sins haunt us any longer! God's grace is what allows us to put our sins behind us. *"Brethren, I count not myself to have apprehended: but this one thing I do, forgetting those things which are behind, and reaching forth unto those things which are before, I press toward the mark for the prize of the high calling of God in Christ Jesus."*—Philippians 3:13–14

Strive to maintain a clear conscience every day of your life. As soon as you have wronged the Lord or someone else, go and ask for forgiveness. The race is much more triumphantly run when sins are forgiven, kept behind us, and forsaken. *"And herein do I exercise myself, to have always a conscience void of offense toward God, and toward men."*—Acts 24:16

Loving God

"And thou shalt love the LORD thy God with all thine heart, and with all thy soul, and with all thy might. And these words, which I command thee this day, shall be in thine heart."—Deuteronomy 6:5–6

Through life, we learn to apply many truths to godly living. We take many steps toward living out God's Word practically, yet this work can be in vain if our hearts are not right, and our relationship with the Lord is not one of love and true service.

When I was about fourteen, our family attended a conference. The topic was "Loving God." To me, it sounded dry and boring. What is there to learn about loving God? As I listened to the messages, however, I felt increasingly convicted of my failure to love the Lord God with all my life. I had been "serving" Him since I could remember, but had I really loved Him? This was an area where I would need gradual improvement.

Many Christians fail to love the Lord Jesus. The problem is that they are so caught up in the obedience part, that they forget to love the One Who created the commandments. How important it is that we desire a close walk with the Father! George Mueller was a man who served his Savior to the fullest. Regardless of his busy days filled with lots of work and service, he never left out the personal, deep relationship that only comes in timely moments with Christ.

> *"I must offer a word of warning* to believers. Often the work of the Lord itself may tempt us away from communion with Him. A full schedule of preaching, counseling, and travel can erode the strength of the mightiest servant of the Lord. Public prayer will never make up for closet communion."
> —George Mueller

God desires us to not only obey Him, but to love Him with all that we are. *"And now, Israel, what doth the LORD thy God require of thee, but to fear the LORD thy God, to walk in all His ways, and to love Him, and to serve the LORD thy God with all thy heart and with all thy soul, to keep the commandments of the LORD, and His statues, which I command thee this day for thy* good?"—Deuteronomy 10:12–13

Just recently I told a child, "If your mother tells you to pick up your toys, the easy part is to do the action. The harder part is doing it with a loving, serving heart and cheerful attitude."

The special thing about loving God is that when one loves the Lord, she desires to please Him, and then the obedience part comes naturally. When a lawyer asked Christ which commandment was the greatest, Jesus answered in this manner: *"Thou shalt love the Lord thy God with all thy heart, and with all thy soul, and with all thy mind. This is the first and great commandment. And the second is like unto it, Thou shalt love thy neighbor as thyself. On these two commandments hang all the law and the prophets."*—Matthew 22:37–40

Study these examples of people who *followed God's "rules,"* but failed to *love* Him with all their lives:

"This people draweth nigh unto Me with their mouth, and honoureth Me with their lips; but their heart is far from Me. But in vain they do worship Me, teaching for doctrines the commandments of men."—Matthew 15:8–9

"I know thy works, and thy labour, and thy patience, and how thou canst not bear them which are evil: and thou hast tried them which say they are apostles, and are not, and hast found them liars: And hast borne, and hast patience, and for my name's sake hast laboured, and hast not fainted. Nevertheless I have somewhat against thee, because thou hast left thy first love."—Revelation 2:2–4

Sadly, these examples describe many of us. Our works are in vain if we do not truly do them with hearts of love and service for the King. When we love Him first, however, the righteous things come easily out of a natural desire to please Him. The Lord rewards those who love Him: *"The LORD preserveth all them that love Him: but all the wicked will He destroy."*—Psalm 145:20

I appreciate Jennifer Lamp's challenge in her book, *His Chosen Bride*:

"Are you resting, content in loving Him today? Not just serving, fearing Him, or obeying Him, but in loving Him. For by focusing on the greater, the lesser will follow naturally as fruit of a right relationship . . . Loving the Lord must be our primary goal as Mark 12:30 exhorts. This is the greatest commandment and the one

from which everything must stem . . . If you are struggling, ask Him to deepen your love for Him. As your love deepens, so the joy in your dedication will multiply."

What You Feed the Most

"Thou therefore endure hardness, as a good soldier of Jesus Christ."
—2 Timothy 2:3

Our pastor told a story about a man who said his life was sometimes like a black dog and a white dog fighting inside of him. When asked, "Which one is winning?" the man answered, "Whichever one I feed the most."

We live in constant battle between flesh and spirit. We have to put on the armor of God and fight against the wiles of the devil. We must be victorious by "feeding" what is good and pure.

"Finally, my brethren, be strong in the Lord, and in the power of His might. Put on the whole armour of God, that ye may be able to stand against the wiles of the devil. For we wrestle not against flesh and blood, but against principalities, against powers, against the rulers of the darkness of this world, against spiritual wickedness in high places. Wherefore take unto you the whole armour of God, that ye may be able to withstand in the evil day, and having done all, to stand. Stand therefore, having your loins girt about with truth, and having on the breastplate of righteousness; And your feet shod with the preparation of the gospel of peace; above all, taking the shield of faith, wherewith ye shall be able to quench all the fiery darts of the wicked. And take the helmet of salvation, and the sword of the Spirit, which is the Word of God."
—Ephesians 6:10–17

On Paper!

I remember a time when I was constantly being asked questions (from people I did and did not know) like, "Aren't you going to college?"

"What do you want to do with your life?" "Do you have any boy friends?" "Why can't you do this or that?"

I was steadfast in what I believed, and I knew the Bible was true. However, sometimes I began to wonder, "Why *do* I believe this? Where *does* the Bible say that?" I felt like I could much better answer curious people's questions if I researched and penned my beliefs, convictions, and reasons why.

"In all things showing thyself a pattern of good works: in doctrine showing uncorruptness, gravity, sincerity, sound speech, that cannot be condemned; that he that is of the contrary part may be ashamed, having no evil thing to say of you."—Titus 2:7–8

"Avoid fruitless arguments and let the truth do all the shouting!"—Bill Gothard

Victory in Jesus

"Now thanks be unto God, which always causeth us to triumph in Christ, and maketh manifest the savour of His knowledge by us in every place."

—2 Corinthians 2:14

Though we fall and stumble, Christ still loves us. His mercy is so wonderful, and His grace is amazing. Through Jesus, we have victory. It is always through the Lord that we are capable of doing His work and becoming daughters of virtue.

We will have troubles along the way, but seek out the Lord and His compassion. He will help you to walk straight and to keep your eyes fixed on Christ. Pray for victory in Jesus. Seek wisdom every day of your life. (See Proverbs 2:1–5.)

Make Jesus Christ your All. He should be all that matters. Abide in Him! (See John 15.)

"Abiding in Christ is a complete surrender of my will to His perfect will. But remember, even the surrender of our will is the work of God, 'For it is God which worketh in you both to will and to do of His good pleasure.' (Philippians 2:13). The only Person who can

> live the Christian life is Jesus Christ. When we set our affections, desires, passions, will, and thoughts on the Person of the Lord Jesus Christ continually, He will live His life through us in an operational or practical way.
>
> "An amazing transformation will happen as you abide in Christ—your life will be full, free, and complete. You will not be sinless. Your life will not suddenly become physically healthy and wealthy, but those things will lose their importance when Christ is supreme in your life. You will find peace in the midst of the storm."
>
> —Forrest Wychopen, in *Abide in Christ*

Do not try to be godly in the flesh because you will be discouraged (and defeated) so quickly! Some of the things I discuss in this book are achievable, practical goals, but I would never want you to think that I am trying to encourage you to work through your flesh, because I know it is a foolish thing to do. Allow the Lord to work through you to have victory over your sins.

Do not be discouraged by things that cause you to stumble—only forsake those sins and ask the Lord's forgiveness. He will grant this desire with loving kindness and everlasting goodness and mercy.

Sisters, yield your life to the One Who gave it to you. Although you may be a born-again believer, you must take up the cross *daily* and follow your Master. Give everything—your desires, plans, goals, hopes, rights, your *life*—to Jesus Christ. When you do this, you will be amazed at the beautiful plan He has for your life, and you will be excited about following it!

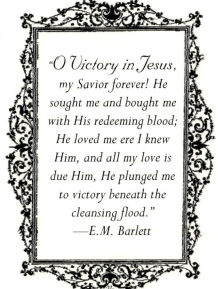

"*O Victory in Jesus*, my Savior forever! He sought me and bought me with His redeeming blood; He loved me ere I knew Him, and all my love is due Him, He plunged me to victory beneath the cleansing flood."
—E.M. Bartlett

There is indeed victory in Jesus!

Noble Girlhood: Becoming a Daughter of Victory & Virtue

Suggested Resources . . .
For books with no contact information, these are available at either your local Christian bookstore, or one of the companies listed under "Godly Resources."

Books:
Stepping Heavenward, by Elizabeth Prentiss
Pilgrim's Progress, by John Bunyan
Princess in Calico, unknown
The Joy of Womanhood, by Suzan Zakula
Jessie Wells, by Isabella Alden
Encouragement for the Missions Heart, compiled by Rachel Sias
(Available from: Rachel Sias—P.O. Box 96, Grandy, MN 55029)

Tapes & CDs:
Bold Christian Youth, by Jonathan Lindvall
(Available from: Bold Christian Living—(559)-539-0500)
Victory for Daughters, by Kelly Brown, Sarah, Rebekah, and Hannah Zes

An Extra Thought . . .

A Good Shepherd

One morning I was reading Luke 12:22–34, one of my favorite passages in the Bible. It reminded me how much I am loved by Jesus Christ, and that I have no reason to be anxious or worried. Do you realize how much God loves you? He calls you His "little flock." *"Fear not, little flock; for it is your Father's good pleasure to give you the kingdom."—Luke 12:32*

I began thinking about Christ our Shepherd, so I flipped over to John 10. (Read verses 7–30 yourself.) What a beautiful picture—to think of Jesus Christ being our Shepherd!

Jesus is the Shepherd; we are the sheep. But Jesus is not an ordinary shepherd; He is the *good* Shepherd—the *good* Shepherd will give His own life for His sheep. *"I am the good Shepherd: the good shepherd giveth his life for the sheep."—John 10:11*

"My sheep hear My voice, and I know them, and they follow Me: And I give unto them eternal life; and they shall never perish, neither shall any man pluck them out of My hand. My Father, which gave them Me, is greater *than all; and no man is able to pluck them out of My Father's hand. I and My Father are one."*—John 10:27–30

So why do we worry, considering what Jesus said in the above verses? Do we realize how compassionate our Lord is? He is God of the universe, yet He gathers His sheep in His arms and takes care of them; He even laid down His life for them. The sheep go astray and get into trouble, yet He leads them back and cares for them.

Jesus' compassion is shown again in John 8. There was a sinful woman, whose penalty was to be stoned. The scribes and Pharisees brought her to Jesus and asked Him what He thought. After some time, Jesus answered, *"He that is without sin among you, let him first cast a stone at her." (verse 7)*

The Bible says that these people were *"convicted by their own conscience" (verse 9)* and left, leaving Jesus and the woman alone. Jesus had been writing on the ground and stood up. *"Woman, where are those thine accusers? Hath no man condemned thee?" "Neither do I condemn thee: go, and sin no more." (verses 10–11)* Jesus *was* the only One without sin, *yet* He Himself *did not* cast a stone.

God has been reminding me to "be anxious for nothing," because He is in control and is taking care of me. When God, the One Who controls my very breath, is caring for me, what more can I ask for? He has also reminded me that He is a loving God—a Shepherd Who loves and lays down His life for His sheep. Even through my sin, foolishness, and disobedience, He shows grace to me, and loves me.

God is so good! Even when we are faithless, He is faithful. Even when we forget Him, He finds us. So often we are like little lambs who continue to wander away from their Shepherd, yet He always picks us up and lovingly places us in His strong, steady, and *certain* arms. Though the world is not certain, though the ground around us may shift, our Savior—our Shepherd—is strong and steady. He protects and comforts us. What an awesome God we have! Let us praise Him for all that He does! *"Some trust in chariots, and some in horses: but we will remember the name of the LORD our God."*—Psalm 20:7

Application...

"But be ye doers of the word, and not hearers only, deceiving your own selves."—James 1:22

What did you learn about victory in Jesus?
_____
_____
_____

List two verses that suggest how to receive victory in the Christian walk:_____
_____

What sins in your life do you need Christ's help to overcome?
_____
_____
_____

Choose one of the following Scriptures to memorize and recite:

Revelation 2:2–4   Hebrews 12:1–3
Proverbs 4:25–27   Psalm 103

Recited to: _____ Date: _____

Choose one of the following activities to work on:

- Write a story or essay about what it means to keep your eyes straight on the right path, not looking to the right or left. (See Proverbs 4.)

- Sit down and make a list of sins you need to clear from your conscience. Pray and ask the Lord to forgive you, then go to anyone you may have wronged, and seek their forgiveness. Read Philippians 3:13–14 and learn how to forgive yourself as well.

–Chapter 11–
Becoming a Daughter of Devotion

"Draw nigh to God, and He will draw nigh to you. Cleanse your hands, ye sinners; and purify your hearts, ye double minded."
—James 4:8

Knowing Jesus Christ by Spending Time with Him

"Sometimes I wonder why I don't feel close to my Savior. I know that I'm saved, but isn't there more to the Christian walk than this?" Grace felt confused.

"Sometimes," Jolene suggested, "I think we don't spend enough time with the Lord. How can we expect to know Him if we spend no time with Him?"

Jolene is right. A girl cannot expect to know her Lord personally if she does not spend time with Him. Just how does she do that?

No Exceptions!

We cannot expect to know Christ if we do not spend time with Him. Suppose you had a pen pal, and she sent you countless letters, but instead of reading them, you simply threw them into a pile of things to do. Could you say you knew her if you never read her letters or corresponded with her? Could you even call her a friend?

You would never do that to your pen pal! Nevertheless, this dreadful situation is actually very common among Christians today. It is not with their friends, but with the most important Friend, the Heavenly Father, our Lord Jesus. Why do Christians treat time with the Lord so lightly? Moreover, just how do Christians expect to know Christ if they never read His great Letter or talk to Him in prayer?

> *"Blessed is the man* that walketh not in the counsel of the ungodly, nor standeth in the way of sinners, nor sitteth in the seat of the scornful. But his delight is in the law of the LORD; and in his law doth he meditate day and night. And he shall be like a tree planted by the rivers of water, that bringeth forth his fruit in his season; his leaf also shall not wither; and whatsoever he doeth shall prosper. The ungodly are not so: but are like the chaff which the wind driveth away. Therefore the ungodly shall not stand in the judgement, nor sinners in the congregation of the righteous. For the LORD knoweth the way of the righteous: but the way of the ungodly shall perish."
>
> —Psalm 1

When comparing the godly with the ungodly, what is the difference? The godly girl spends time in God's Word and with Him. She *delights* in spending time with the Lord, and she meditates on His promises.

There are no exceptions! If you desire a strong walk with the Lord, and long to know Him better, time with Him is *vital every day*.

A Chore or an Opportunity?

"O GOD, Thou art my God; early will I seek Thee: my soul thirsteth for Thee, my flesh longeth for Thee in a dry and thirsty land, where no water is; to see Thy power and Thy glory, so as I have seen Thee in the sanctuary. Because Thy lovingkindness is better than life, my lips shall praise Thee."

—Psalm 63:1–3

Years ago, I established a daily quiet time with the Lord. For the most part, I have had this time with Him every day. However, I can remember a dry part in my Christian walk when these moments with God had become a chore instead of an opportunity.

I woke up and thought, "Okay, I've got lots to do, but I have to do my Bible study first, so . . . one Psalm should cover that," which would be followed by a hasty prayer.

Let me challenge you: Is your time with the Lord a chore on your "to-do" list, or an opportunity to grow in Him and get to know Him better?

This special time with our heavenly Father is to be an opportunity to grow closer to Him, not another thing you "have to" accomplish that day. What is our heart's true desire?

"O how love I Thy law! It is my meditation all the day. Thou through Thy commandments hast made me wiser than mine enemies: for they are ever with me. I have more understanding than all my teachers: for Thy testimonies are my meditation. I understand more than the ancients, because I keep Thy precepts. I have refrained my feet from every evil way, that I might keep Thy word. I have not departed from Thy judgments: for Thou hast taught me. How sweet are Thy words unto my taste! Yea, sweeter than honey to my mouth! Through Thy precepts I get understanding: therefore I hate every false way." —Psalm 119:97–104*

Is this what you long for? To read God's Word so often that your mind is filled with its treasures? Do you strive to know God better? There is no better time to begin studying the Bible than now!

Peace and Quiet

"Satan will always find you something to do when you ought to be occupied about that [prayer and Bible study], if it is only arranging a window blind."
—J. Hudson Taylor

Sometimes my quiet time is lacking one important quality: quietness!☺ You know how it is in the middle of the day at times—the little ones are asking for oatmeal, someone decided to play the piano, and the phone just rang for the billionth time! How are we to study God's Word in such an atmosphere?

First, we cannot make this an excuse to miss quiet time all together. However, we have to *improvise* and make things work. A few things that have helped my quiet time stay *quiet* would include having my studies in the morning while most of the family is still in bed, having it outside in God's creation (this is a neat thing to do!), having it in my bedroom, the list goes on! Be creative!

It is important that your quiet time is quiet because it is hard to seek God and His will when concentration is not achievable. However, even more importantly is the condition of your heart. Is your heart at peace and quiet? Or are you nervous or anxious? These things also effect the results of your time with God.

Before you begin reading God's Word, pray. Ask the Lord to calm down your soul and teach you. Ask Him what He wants you to learn that particular day. *"Speak, LORD; for thy servant heareth."*—1 Samuel 3:9b

"Have you . . . thus learned to use your eyes? *Do you know that the eyes of your mind are naturally darkened, so that you can neither read with understanding the . . . book of God's Word: When David prays, 'Open mine eyes, that I may see the wonderful things out of thy law,' he speaks of the eyes of the mind, which must be opened before the Bible can be rightly understood; and in the*

same way we must pray to God to open our eyes before we can see Him in His works, and learn the lessons He has inscribed upon them. If your eyes are not yet opened . . . you are losing a rich source of pleasure, as well as profit. Pray to God to open them, and then go into the free air, with the Bible for your interpreter, and read the lessons. Listen to hear the still small voice that speaks . . . and if you once hear it, you will find the enjoyment so sweet, you will ever wish to hear it again, you will love it more than can be told, you will wonder at your former blindness." —The Basket of Flowers, by J. H. St. A.

No Better Time than Now

"Wherewithal shall a young man cleanse his way? by taking heed thereto according to Thy word. With my whole heart have I sought thee: O let me not wander from Thy commandments. Thy word have I hid in mine heart, that I might not sin against Thee. Blessed art Thou, O LORD: teach me Thy statutes . . . I will meditate in Thy precepts, and have respect unto Thy ways. I will delight myself in Thy statutes: I will not forget Thy word." —Psalm 119:9–12, 15–16

It seems that the older I get, the busier I get. How grateful I am that I formed the habit of a daily quiet time when I was little! It is a normal part of my everyday life now, and has been a tremendous help in my spiritual growth.

The best time to begin studying God's Word and seeking His wisdom is in your youth. Right now, though you may go through busy times, you are at one of the most fragile and calmest parts of your life. During your youth, you can best learn God's ways and His righteousness.

It has been said that a person is most impressionable during his years before eighteen. By reading God's Word as a young person, you are building your life on a solid foundation, and it will not be easily shaken. A person who learns these principles while he is still young has a promising future.

Many think, "When I get married, I will have more time for God." Or, "When I graduate, I will have more time for God." This may seem true, but talk to your mom! ☺ Use your single years for God and His glory. Do not waste them doing things of temporary value; get to know Him better so that when you do enter marriage, you will already have that advantage.

"But I would have you without carefulness. He that is unmarried careth for the things that belong to the Lord, how he may please the Lord: but he that is married careth for the things that are of the world, how he may please his wife. There is difference also between a wife and a virgin. The unmarried woman careth for the things of the Lord, that she may be holy both in body and in spirit: but she that is married careth for the things of the world, how she may please her husband."—1 Corinthians 7:32–34

This passage is not saying that it is a sin to be married, or that marriage is not encouraged among Christians. The Bible is clear that marriage is a part of God's plan. However, these verses do challenge us to use the years of our youth to get to know God better that we may be godlier women (and possibly wives) of the future. The more we know God and His ways, the more we are like Him, and the more virtuous we become.

"The PROVERBS of Solomon the son of David, king of Israel; to know wisdom and instruction; to perceive the words of understanding; to receive the instruction of wisdom, justice, and judgment, and equity; to give subtlety to the simple, to the young man knowledge and discretion. A wise man will hear, and will increase learning; and a man of understanding shall attain unto wise counsels."—Proverbs 1:1–5

Many girls in their teenage years have questions about Scriptural matters. What does God say about this? Does He want me to do this or that? Is this thing a sin? Am I supposed to do this? All these questions a young girl has can be answered by the Lord Himself, and He will guide her, if she will only seek Him through prayer and His Word.

Do not hesitate to use the years of your youth to soak your mind into the Scriptures. Learn all you can while you have your parents to guide you. One day, you will see the benefits of using this time in your life to grow in the Lord and build a lasting foundation on Him. It will bless your future immensely!

More than Words

The Bible is more than a few words joined together to make sentences. It is a letter of love from the Heavenly Father written especially to you. The messages in it are new in each chapter, prophecies fill the pages, and wisdom is woven through each verse. By viewing the Bible as God's Words to you, you will come to understand and appreciate it more. *"All Scripture is given by inspiration of God, and is profitable for doctrine, for reproof, for correction, for instruction in righteousness: That the man of God may be perfect, thoroughly furnished unto all good works."—2 Timothy 3:16–17*

These words are not man's insights. This Letter is the work of the Lord, inspired by God, and men simply put His Words on paper. One of God's purposes in writing the Bible was to instruct us in righteousness. We are accountable to His Word because His righteous ways are on paper, and we have no excuse for violating them.

If I want to communicate something of great importance to you, and I want you to never forget or forsake what I say, I will not pick up the telephone and call you to talk about it. I will not invite you over for lunch and explain it. Carefully and thoughtfully, I will write it out—so that you will always be able to look back at it any time you wish or need to.

This is what God wanted for us. A Letter that would explain His plan for salvation, His purpose for our lives, how we can live according to His ways, how to be like Him, and a record of

---

My Old Bible

Though the cover is worn,
and the pages are torn,
And though places bear traces of tears,
Yet more precious than gold
Is this book worn and old,
That can shatter and scatter my fears.

This old Book is my guide,
'Tis a friend by my side,
It will lighten and brighten my way;
And each promise I find
Soothes and gladdens the mind,
As I read it and heed it each day.

To this book I will cling,
Of its worth I will sing,
Tho' great losses and crosses be mine;
For I cannot despair,
Though surrounded by care,
While possessing this blessing divine.

who Jesus Christ was (and is). A humorous but truthful acronym for "Bible" is "**B**asic **I**nstructions **B**efore **L**eaving **E**arth."

So this Book that God has given you is not a mere book; it is the Word of God. It is brimming full of His ways and His righteousness. By reading it, you will come to know God and His plan and purpose for your life with a greater understanding.

"Carefully read the Word and meditate on it. Through reading the Word of God, and especially through meditation on it, the believer becomes acquainted with the nature and character of God. Besides God's holiness and justice, he realizes what a kind, loving, gracious, merciful, mighty, wise, and faithful Father He is. Therefore, in poverty, affliction, death of loved ones, difficulty in service, or financial need, he will rest on the ability of God to help him. He has learned from the Word that God is almighty in power, infinite in wisdom, and ready to help and deliver His people. Reading the Word of God, together with meditation on it, is an excellent way to strengthen faith."

—George Mueller

The Search is On!

"Give therefore Thy servant an understanding heart to judge Thy people, that I may discern between good and bad . . . And the speech pleased the Lord, that Solomon had asked this thing. And all Israel heard of the judgment which the king had judged; and they feared the king: for they saw that the wisdom of God was in him, to do judgment." —1 Kings 3:9–10, 28

Do you search for wisdom as King Solomon did? I remember at a young age learning the story of Solomon—his longing for wisdom and the many earthly possessions God granted him because of his godly desire. My initial thought was what many children probably first think, "Wow! Maybe if I ask God for wisdom, He will give me lots of money, books, and all sorts of stuff I like!" ☺

I even remember praying and asking the Lord to grant me wisdom (in hopes of earthly treasures), but on this particular subject the wisdom came a little later. Now, today, I would choose wisdom over any amount of money or any earthly possession. Wisdom is priceless, and while many people are born smart, no one is born wise. It is not a part of human nature—we are naturally fools and sinners. *"Foolishness is bound in the heart of a child; but the rod of correction shall drive it far from him."—Proverbs 22:15* God grants wisdom to those who seek it.

> *"Many years ago, my father admonished me to pray for God's wisdom every single day. Those words have stayed with me and I praise the Lord for His clear direction as He has answered these prayers! This godly advice I pass along to you, dear sisters. James 1:5 'If any of you lack wisdom, let him ask of God.'"*
>
> —Tara Riddell, in *Virtuous Daughters*

"Get wisdom, get understanding: forget it not; neither decline from the words of my mouth. Forsake her not, and she shall preserve thee: love her, and she shall keep thee. Wisdom is the principal thing; therefore get wisdom: and with all thy getting get understanding. Exalt her, and she shall promote thee: she shall bring thee to honour, when thou dost embrace her. She shall give to thine head an ornament of grace: a crown of glory shall she deliver to thee."
—*Proverbs 4:5–9*

By seeking God and His Word daily and *wholeheartedly*, we will obtain wisdom. It is more than just "skimming through" the Bible; Proverbs tell us that we must seek wisdom as silver and search for it as hidden treasures. *"Then shalt thou understand the fear of the LORD, and find the knowledge of God."—Proverbs 2:5*

The Bible promises that if we are truly seeking wisdom we will find it. Search God's Word and His ways, and you will be a wise daughter of the Truth!

Applying the Wisdom

There is a memory from about five or six years ago that has changed the way I have my quiet time each day. It was a nice day and my brother and I were talking about having a Bible study. I said to him with a hint of pride in my voice, "Well, my day always goes better when I have my Bible study in the morning. I make fewer foolish mistakes, and I am more aware of doing what is right."

A few days later, Justin and I were arguing about something in the schoolroom. He asked me in the thick of it, "Did you have your Bible study today?!" His question caught me off guard, and I was a little surprised.

"Yes, why?"

"Because, you said the other day that when you have your Bible study you make fewer mistakes and are more aware of doing right."

What a revelation! I had read a passage of Scripture that morning, but I had sadly failed to learn from it, to apply the wisdom that I could have very well used that day!

Most of us are probably guilty of "skimming through" our quiet time at times. We are in a hurry, and we fail to learn the messages that are not on the surface of the words. This is a bad habit, and we must overcome it with meditation, patience, and dedication to the Word of God.

> "But be ye doers of the Word, and not hearers only, deceiving your own selves. For if any be a hearer of the word, and not a doer, he is like unto a man beholding his natural face in a glass: For he beholdeth himself, and goeth his way, and straightway forgetteth what manner of man he was. But whoso looketh into the perfect law of liberty, and continueth therein, he being not a forgetful hearer, but a doer of the work, this man shall be blessed in his deed."—James 1:22–25

When you read the Word of God, *study it*. Apply it to your life. Decipher through it to discover the message that lies underneath. You will be amazed at the blessings of reading, studying, and applying the treasures and wisdom in the Bible.

Sometimes it can be especially hard to study what you are reading if you have no accountability. My brother encouraged me to journal my Bible studies—to write about what I learned each day. It is a refreshing thing to look back on, and the journaling helps the wisdom you attained to become a part of your life.

Each Day, Each Minute

Do not just spend time with the Lord when you feel like it or on Sunday. Make Jesus a part of your life. Make prayer a part of your life. Make His Word a part of your life. These things should soon become habits and pleasures that you delight in so much!

The time specifically set aside for just God will vary with each Christian. You can decide this with the Lord's guidance. However, do not simply spend thirty minutes or one hour with the Lord every morning, but leave Him out of everything else. Make Him and His Word a part of every minute. As you come to know Him better, this will become more evident in your life.

Also, just because you have a certain time chosen for your quiet time does not mean you cannot flee to Him in prayer or in His Word any time or part of the day. Very often in our family, when someone brings up a certain subject or topic, one of us might go get our Bible to clarify a statement or point out a truth. This brings God's Word into our lives on a regular basis.

We have already concluded that if we want to know God better, it is vital to spend time with Him. Make this your goal and challenge—to know God better and to spend more time with Him this year and forever.

"The Bible contains the mind of God, the state of man, the way of salvation, the doom of sinners, and the happiness of believers. Its doctrines are holy, its precepts are binding, its histories are true, and its decisions are immutable. Read it to be wise, believe it to be safe, and practice it to be holy. It contains light to direct you, food to support you, and comfort to cheer you.

"It is the traveler's map, the pilgrim's staff, the pilot's compass, the soldier's sword, and the Christian's charter. Here Paradise is restored, Heaven opened, and the gates of hell disclosed.

"CHRIST is its grand subject, our good the design, and the glory of God its end.

"It should fill the memory, rule the heart, and guide the feet. Read it slowly, frequently, and prayerfully. It is a mine of wealth, a paradise of glory, and a river of pleasure. It is given you in life, will be opened at the judgment, and be remembered forever. It involves the highest responsibility, will reward the greatest labor, and will condemn all who trifle with its sacred contents." —The Gideons International

Before the Throne of Grace
"Let us therefore come boldly unto the throne of grace, that we may obtain mercy, and find grace to help in time of need." —Hebrew 4:16

I must admit that I struggle more with talking to God through prayer than listening to Him by reading the Bible. It may be that I am not as much of a talker as some people are. The excuse for my weakness, however, is aside from the fact that prayer is to be exercised just as reading the Bible is.

Prayer is a major factor in the Christian walk. As we search the Scriptures, we find that God's greatest servants were those who went to Him in time of need, and let Him comfort them. By reading the Bible, we are learning God's will for our lives, but it is important to communicate with Him too. This is another way of spending time with the Father. *"Pray without ceasing."*—1 Thessalonians 5:17

"And the prayer of faith shall save the sick, and the Lord shall raise him up; and if he have committed sins, they shall be forgiven him. Confess your faults one to another, and pray one for another, that ye may be healed. The effectual prayer of a righteous man availeth much. Elias was a man subject to like passions as we are, and he prayed earnestly that it might not rain: and it rained not on the earth by the space of three years and six months. And he prayed again, and the heaven gave rain, and the earth brought forth her fruit."
—James 5:15–18

For me, the best way to share my burdens with God and come to Him with praise, gratitude, trouble, or distress, is to write to Him! It is a neat thing to do because I can look back at prayers I prayed in my own diary. This way of prayer has greatly helped my Christian walk, though I will add that I also pray to Him verbally throughout the day, because that is important too.

I have always thought it so refreshing to think that we can pray to a living God Who will actually hear and answer our prayers! There are some who have ritual prayer times each day, yet they pray to false gods, or people who are dead and do not hear them. Their hours of prayers are never heard, and certainly never answered. Praise God for His listening ear!

> *"The mystery of prayer! There is nothing like it in the natural universe . . . Marvelous bond of prayer which can span the gulf between the Creator and the creature, the infinite God and the humblest and most illiterate child!"*
>
> —A.B. Simpson, founder of Christian and missionary alliance

When I think of a true prayer warrior, my mother is the first to come to mind. She has always gone to the Lord for physical needs, comfort, guidance, and wisdom. She has cried out to God for the saving of souls and His provision for our family. Although I could fill up many pages writing about different requests that God has mysteriously answered, I will just say it is amazing and exciting to see how He has worked through her prayers. Thank you for the godly example you have set for me of a true prayer warrior, Mommy! ♥

Spend time with the Lord, and you will know Him better. The only way that you can make Jesus Christ your best friend and closest companion is if you talk with Him, read His Letter to you, and build an every day, every minute relationship. If you do not already have this special time established, do not hesitate one minute. Start today! *"As the hart panteth after the water brooks, so panteth my soul after Thee, O God. My soul thirsteth for God, for the living God: when shall I come and appear before God?"*—Psalm 42:1–2

Suggested Resources . . .

Books:
Abide in Christ, by Forrest Wychopen
Waiting for Her Isaac, by Mr. and Mrs. Stephen B. Castleberry
The Hymnal

An Extra Thought . . .

The Life of Prayer
Taken from *Virtuous Daughters,* by Mrs. Cheryl Schlichter

For most girls, talking comes easily. Praying is just talking to our Heavenly Father. My favorite prayers to learn from were David's because he candidly prayed from his heart to his Father. I think of how he spent so much time alone caring for his earthly father's sheep, yet he was never really alone. He had the best companionship that anyone can have. I have learned from the prayers of David that I can share from the depths of my heart with my Father. He knows my thoughts, but why not take the time to share them with Him?

Girls, there is no one else who can be with you always, or love you so deeply as God. Tell him your every concern, your thankfulness, and ask His forgiveness when you've sinned. *"The Lord is nigh unto all them that call upon Him, to all that call upon Him in truth."—Psalm 145:18* Won't you spend some time right now talking to the Lord?

Application . . .

"But be ye doers of the word, and not hearers only, deceiving your own selves."—James 1:22

Do you have a daily quiet time established? If not, establish one now; what time will you do it? Where? What will you read?

_____
_____
_____
_____

List two Scriptures that focus on *time with God*: _____
_____
_____

Choose one of the following Scriptures to memorize and recite:

James 5:15–18   *Psalm 1*
2 Timothy 3:16–17   *Psalm 119:97–104*
Proverbs 1:1–5   *James 4:8*

Recited to:_____ Date: _____

Choose one of the following activities to work on:

- Buy a journal, and record your Bible study notes and specific prayers each day as you have time with God.

- Find one verse from each passage of Scripture you read and copy it onto a note card; throughout the day work to memorize and apply it.

- Find a friend or family member to hold you accountable (and you hold them accountable) for Bible reading. Each week share with each other what you learned.

–Chapter III–
Becoming a Daughter of Purpose

"Let your light so shine before men, that they may see your good works, and glorify your Father which is in Heaven."
—Matthew 5:16

Learning God's Purpose for My Life
And Serving Him with Motivation and Dedication

"What on earth am I here for?" Susan asked her friend Lacy.

"I don't know—I suppose we're here to have fun." Lacy exclaimed as she threw her hat across the room. "But, on a second thought, why are we here? Surely, there is more to my life than just enjoying myself. Oh well, let's go shopping."

What these girls lack is purpose! God does have a purpose for every young person. But what is that special, unique plan?

The Light of the World

"Ye are our epistle written in our hearts, known and read of all men: forasmuch as ye are manifestly declared to be the epistle of Christ ministered by us, written not with ink, but with the Spirit of the living God; not in tables of stone, but in fleshy tables of the heart."   —2 Corinthians 3:2–3

Countless girls have had thoughts something like this: "I don't know why I'm here; I don't know what I'm to do with my life. How can God use me?"

I have news for you—news from the Lord. He does have a very special purpose for you! He put you here for a special reason! He loves you, and He can use you in ways you cannot begin to imagine!

"Ye are the salt of the earth: but if the salt have lost his savour, wherewith shall it be salted? It is thenceforth good for nothing, but to be cast out, and to be trodden under foot of men. Ye are the light of the world. A city that is set on a hill cannot be hid. Neither do men light a candle, and put it under a bushel, but on a candlestick; and it giveth light unto all that are in the house. Let your light so shine before men, that they may see your good works, and glorify your Father which is in heaven."   —Matthew 5:13–16

Do we realize the importance of this Scripture? We are the salt of the earth—but so many Christians have lost their savor, resulting in an "unsalted" earth. As young women growing in an unsalted earth, we ought to be sure that we are full of savor, full of Christ's love. We are to be making an effort to "salt the earth" before it is too late.

Countless girls do not realize that they are the salt of the earth, the light of the world. They fail to understand that the reason God has them here right now is to bring glory and honor to His name. Every Christian has a life purpose. Your purpose for life lies right here in the Scripture—you are to honor and bring glory to Jesus Christ.

"So what does that mean for me, personally?" you may question. "How can I bring glory to God's name? How can I know specifically what His purpose for my life is?"

A Willing Heart

We must remember that we begin fulfilling our life purpose when we give our lives to Christ . . . when we say, "Lord, I am Yours. I am Your tool; I am willing to do whatever You have in store for me." The same principle holds true in a poem my brother wrote:

> *"You are the Potter, I am the clay;*
> *What do You want me to do today?"*
>
> —Justin Schlichter

Let us take some examples of girls who scarcely realized what impact they would have on others as they diligently yielded to God's will, waiting to do His work.

Jenny Lind, a Swedish girl in the 1800s, simply sang to her pet cat in her grandmother's house, day by day. It had never occurred to her that the Lord would one day use her beautiful voice for His glory in mighty ways as she sang with a heart for the Lord.

Sarah F. Adams was unaware that the Lord would turn some of her greatest disappointments into triumph. Although she had wanted to teach religious truths on stage, God had a different plan. She but little realized as she wrote the well-loved hymn, "Nearer my God, to Thee," that it would have an influence on millions of lives.

Ida Lewis, a young woman of fifteen, as she rowed her brothers and sister to and from school at their lighthouse home, could not imagine the many lives she would save from drowning because she was yielded to God and her parents' wishes at a young age.

I wonder if some of these girls thought the same thing many girls think today—"What is God's purpose for me in life? Why am I not doing something 'great' for His glory? How is He going to use me?" Instead of trying to follow the world's view of "purpose" (live for yourself), they selflessly waited on the Lord, constantly yielding to Him. Look at the doors He opened for them, all because they were willing.

"I wasn't God's first choice for what I've done for China . . . I don't know who it was . . . It must have been a man . . . a well-educated man. I don't know what happened. Perhaps he died. Perhaps he wasn't wiling . . . And God looked down . . . and saw Gladys Aylward . . . And God said—'Well, she's willing!'"

—Gladys Aylward, missionary to China

We Must Have Purpose

It is very difficult to live a life and not have a purpose. It is like walking down a road with no goal in sight. Bring purpose into your life! What is our purpose? Our life purpose is to bring honor and glory to Christ's name and to be tools for His work. Do not set your purpose to the side; pursue it and strive to fulfill it!

As you yield to God's will, and maintain a selfless, loving spirit, God can work through you to make a difference in others' lives. I would like to remind you that the word "purpose" does not have to frighten you. "I'm too busy

> If you want to make a difference in the world, you have to go in a different direction than the world.

to have a purpose in life! I'm doing school, helping with dinner, and trying to keep up writing my pen pals!"

If helping your mother with dinner and encouraging fellow sisters in the Lord is something that occupies you, do you realize that you are already fulfilling your life purpose? As long as the activities and things you are doing are honoring the Lord, and you are serving Him with a willing heart, you are at a wonderful place in your life!

I think many girls ponder the question, "Is it bad to do things just for pleasure every once in a while? Is it okay if I do not have an outside ministry, but simply help around the house? Is it sin to read a story that is not Christian, but just for fun?" I really enjoyed a good answer to this in the wonderful book, *Stepping Heavenward*:

> "*The most indifferent actions* cease to be such and become good as soon as one performs them with the intention of conforming one's self in them to the will of God. They are often better and purer than certain actions that appear more virtuous. 1st, because they are less of our own choice and more in the order of Providence when one is obliged to perform them; 2nd, because they are simpler and less exposed to vain complaisance; 3rd, because if one yields to them with moderation, one finds in them more of death to one's inclinations than in certain acts of fervor in which self-love mingles; finally, because these little occasions occur more frequently and furnish a secret occasion for continually making every moment profitable.
>
> "It is not necessary to make great efforts nor acts of great reflection in order to offer what are called indifferent actions. It is enough to lift the soul one instant to God, to make a simple offering of it. Everything which God wishes us to do, and which enters into the course of occupation suitable to our position, can and ought to be offered to God; nothing is unworthy of Him but sin. When you feel that an action cannot be offered to God, conclude that it does not become a Christian; it is at least necessary to suspect it and seek light concerning it. I would not have a special prayer for each of these things; the elevation of the heart at the moment suffices.

"As for visits, commissions and the like, as there is danger of following one's own taste too much, I would add to this elevating of the heart a prayer for grace to moderate myself and use precaution."

While we are all here to bring glory to God's name, He does not have everyone baking bread for the homeless three times a week! He likes variety, and His work would not be complete if each of us did not have a similar but different purpose. God chooses for some of His servants to be on the fields of a foreign land, preaching the Gospel, some to be baking bread, some to be encouraging others through conferences or writings, and others to serve within the walls of their own homes.

While one of Sarah Adams's ministries in life was to write for the Lord's glory, Ida Lewis was saving lives from drowning. Jenny Lind was bringing honor to the Lord by her frequent singing, whether it was to a sick person in the hospital, or to a crowd of eager listeners. Then, of course, there was Mary in the Bible. What was her purpose in life? God did not forget her either. She was to raise the long-awaited Savior. Mary is an excellent example of a godly woman with a willing heart.

Neither has the Lord forgotten you. Are you willing to submit to God's will in all things? If so, then He is ready to use you as one of His tools. May the joy of the Lord be your strength! (See Nehemiah 8:10.)

Our life purpose is quite clear—to bring glory to the Father in Heaven. One of the reasons that many Christians are taking after the world is because they cannot find their purpose in life. When a girl cannot find her purpose, she does what everyone else is doing. Sadly, the world's motto, "live for yourself," is not the right thing, and God is displeased with the way many worldly Christian young people are acting.

We are called to be different! We are to live for Christ! We are to have purpose in life! Our motto is so contrary, so opposite to that of the world. Let us not be ashamed, however, for our purpose is beautiful, and we will be rewarded in Heaven on that glorious day.

Would you like to find a specific ministry that honors God? Let's get started! As we said earlier, the Lord has each of us here for His glory. In finding a specific ministry He has for you, you must seek your parents' counsel, pray, and spend time in the Word. God gives each of us a purpose and ministry for our lives.

Working through Circumstances

"The more obstacles you have, the more opportunities there are for God to do something." —Clarence W. Jones

Please keep in mind that before we pursue any kind of a commitment, we must be certain that we are in the center of the Lord's will. God often keeps young women in their home to serve the people He has placed first in their lives, and then occasionally gives them a second "ministry" that is smaller, and serving those outside of her home. Talk to your parents before taking on any kind of a regular commitment. "Do you think that by starting this bread ministry I will be neglecting other people and responsibilities God has placed in my life?" Remember that our ultimate purpose is to bring glory to God's name. (See Matthew 5:16.) *"Whether therefore ye eat, or drink, or whatsoever ye do, do all to the glory of God."*—1 Corinthians 10:31

"But it should be understood that for every wife the first duty is the making and keeping of her own home. Her first and best work should be done there, and till it is well done she has no right to go outside to take up other duties. She is to be a 'worker at home.' She must look upon her home as the one spot on earth for which she alone is responsible, and which she must cultivate well for God if she never does anything outside. For her the Father's business is not attending Dorcas societies and missionary meetings, and mothers' meetings, and temperance conventions, or even teaching a Sunday-school class, until she has made her own home all that her wisest thought and best skill can make it. There have been wives who in their zeal for Christ's work outside have neglected Christ's work inside their own doors. They have had eyes and hearts for human need and human sorrow in the broad fields lying far out, but neither eye nor heart for the work of love lain about their own feet. The result has been that while they were doing angelic work in the lanes and streets, the angels were mourning over their neglected duties within the hallowed walls of their own homes. While they were winning a place in the hearts of the

poor or the sick or the orphan, they were losing their rightful place in the hearts of their own household. Let it be remembered that Christ's work in the home is the first that He gives to every wife, and that no amount of consecrated activities in other spheres will atone in this world or the next for neglect or failure there."

—J. R. Miller, in *Home-Making*

A dear friend shared with me a verse in a way that I had never seen it. *"The king's heart is in the hand of the LORD, as the rivers of water: he turneth it whithersoever he will."*—Proverbs 21:1 She suggested replacing "king's" with "parents.'" Just because I think that a bread ministry is a wonderful opportunity and ministry, if my parents are uncomfortable with such a plan, I must trust the Lord to use me in a different way. I would definitely not be honoring the Lord if I were not honoring my parents. God does speak through our parents!

You see, God can work through us no matter what the circumstances. I think of Fanny Crosby. Even through her blindness, God used her greatly for His glory. Maybe you are afraid that by simply completing schoolwork assignments and helping your mother you are not doing much for His glory. Do not let Satan deceive you with such a lie! *"Ye are our epistle written in our hearts, known and read of all men: Forasmuch as ye are manifestly declared to be the epistle of Christ ministered by us, written not with ink, but with the Spirit of the living God; not in tables of stone, but in fleshy tables of the heart."*—2 Corinthians 3:2–3

Some of the people God has used greatest in my life have been those who have a heart for the Lord, and selflessly serve Him in an every day manner. Take my mother for example: she has a gift of writing, but as she reminds me when I tell her she should start a magazine for moms ☺, this is not the time the Lord has for her to do that right now. At present, her mission field is the hearts of her children and her ministry is in the home. Right now, you may have the same mission field: your home, serving your parents, and being an example to and loving your siblings.

If God is calling you to minister strictly in the home, you can probably come up with a small way of ministering to your family in addition to doing every day service. I think of my sweet five-year old brother. Already, he is using the gifts God has given Him to glorify Him! Gideon loves music and he is learning to play the piano. He excitedly plays God-honoring hymns at recitals, and enjoys blessing his family members on their birthday with a special song. My thirteen-year old brother does many things each day, but one of them is opening our gate each time we leave or come to the house. He has been so loyal in this duty, and it is a blessing to us! These seemingly small acts of service are actually ministries for my brothers that honor the Lord.

Also, remember that if God does not allow you to do one thing that seems good, He has something better in store! When we looked at property in Buffalo, and Trinity, Texas, we liked a couple of pieces in particular. Both were out of our price range, however, and it was not the right timing. As a family, we remembered that God had something better for us waiting if we were patient.

Finding a Ministry

Remember to shift the focus from *you* to *God*. What does *He* want you to be doing? Too often in the process of ministering, our focus is on the flesh. It ought to be on Christ working through us.

> *"To ask, 'What is my calling?' is to ask the wrong question. The right question is, 'LORD, where did You create me to join You where You are working?' Move the focus off 'me', unto 'LORD,' and find His purpose for creating you! It's a relief, and settles a lot of needless confusion."*
> —T. Comp

If you feel God is calling you to a ministry that does require a commitment and you have your parents' blessing, then that is wonderful! I would like to encourage you to start seeking God's will for exactly what that means for you. Here are some practical pointers:

❧ What spiritual gift has God given you? _____

☙ What other (practical) gifts has the Lord granted you? *(Are you skilled in the kitchen; has He given you a beautiful voice; Do you excel in the field of writing, sewing, etc.?)*_____
_____
_____

☙ What "group of people" has the Lord given you "a heart for"? *(My mother has always had a heart for the homeless; I have a heart for younger girls; maybe yours is missionaries; etc.)*_____
_____
_____

☙ In what ways can you use the gifts God has given you for His glory? Remember to allow the Lord to work *through* you! *(If you are a great cook, there may be a ministry to bake bread for the homeless available; the opportunities are numerous!)*_____
_____

☙ Take each step slowly. If writing is your interest, then start by writing edifying stories for your siblings. God may never desire for you to be a published author. One friend of mine had a birthday ministry. Each Sunday at church she would jot down the birthday list and mail birthday notes to each lady who had a birthday that week. Seek Him as you follow His guiding.

❧ For those of you who do not feel God is calling you to start a "commitment ministry," all the above questions apply to you as well. You just have to think in different terms. ☺ God wants to use you, no matter what the circumstances. He may not have you going to Africa, but the plan He does have for you is very important and you must cheerfully accept it like a true servant does. Things like writing stories for your siblings, helping your sister with her school work, setting an example for and loving other girls, sewing for your mom, encouraging your father, building a strong relationship with your siblings, babysitting your neighbor's children—all of these may seem trivial to you, but God will use them in marvelous ways. *"And they that be wise shall shine as the brightness of the firmament; and they that turn many to righteousness as the stars for ever and ever."—Daniel 12:3*

Of course, your ministry begins in your home, and for a woman, often stays there, as we previously talked about. Consider what Sarah Mally, author of *Making Brothers and Sisters Best Friends*, says about ministry:

> *"God has given each of us* the perfect place to learn to be a servant: at home! Everyday there are many opportunities for us to serve our parents and brothers and sisters. Actually, home is the most difficult place to serve, so I think that if we learn to be a servant in our own family, we will be able to be a servant anywhere. <u>We must not reject this first assignment from the Lord by asking for a better one</u>." (emphasis added)

Please strive to fulfill the purpose God has given you—to bring glory and honor to His name. Make this your ultimate goal and greatest achievement in life. Especially during your youth, it is important to use those sweet years to serve the Father in specific ways.

Remember that God's greatest servants were those who began with willing, loving, and serving hearts. Keep in mind that God can use your weaknesses for His glory, too. (Why? Christ is working *through* you—you are simply a tool!)

When God Gave Me a Ministry . . .

At the age of twelve, I wanted to do something with my life. I was beginning to grow up, and childish games and toys became dry and boring. I felt that I must have something more important to do with the gift of life God had given me.

Because I loved to write, my parents encouraged me to use that skill for God's glory in some way. Through much prayer, they encouraged my starting a monthly newsletter titled *Virtuous Daughters* for young ladies to encourage them in the Lord. Although my parents covered the expenses, I had the joy of taking a blank document and prayerfully filling it with inspiring poems, Scriptures, and articles. God blessed the newsletter, as it has grown in size and in number of participants, and is still in print today.

God used this gift of writing because I used it for His honor and glory. (Thanks to my parents for their constant encouragement in that area!) Each month as I work on *Virtuous Daughters*, I must remind myself that I am an instrument doing it to the honor and praise of my Savior. If I do it for my own benefit or value, the work is in vain and will crumble quickly.

Another thing I have to be careful of is my attitude. Sometimes doing *Virtuous Daughters* is just a chore, when it should be an opportunity to encourage others in the Lord! I should view this as such a rare privilege to honor my Savior! The best way for me to do this is to constantly pray and ask God to bless the ministry, as well as keep my focus by reading the Scriptures.

God has given you a special gift or talent. Do you use it for His glory? Or have you neglected and forgotten it? If so, you are missing many opportunities to glorify God with that gift. Do not be like the servant in Matthew 25 who hid his talent and chose not to honor his lord with that gift.

I do not mean by this that every girl should start a big ministry, but you can use your gift in a small ministry under your parents' guidance. Two of my friends are gifted in cooking, and they willingly and lovingly serve their parents by making meals. Holly is responsible for every meal. Another friend, Brianna, does a majority of the cooking when her mother is unable to. She is also skilled in the area of sewing, and she uses this gift to honor God by making clothes for her family.

Keep in mind that one of the best ways to glorify God with your talents is to serve your family with that talent because He will one day desire you to do that for your future husband. By serving your parents with your gifts, you help to further their ministry.

Other ideas for ministry are:

- *Sewing for your family and others in times of need*
- *Meals for your family and others in times off need*

- Reading to small children
- Writing edifying short stories for siblings and friends
- Singing at church or in assisted living homes
- Babysitting your younger siblings or other children in time of need (Note: I think many girls do not realize how much of a blessing it is when they baby-sit! By having an open schedule to watch your younger siblings when your parents are away, you are being a huge blessing!)
- Encouraging pen pals in the Lord through letters
- Praying for different people each day
- Use your unique talents to glorify God in a unique way! ♥

Remember that you do not have to do something "big" to glorify God. I think of God's servant Job. What an awesome man he was and how much he glorified the Lord! It was not anything in particular that he did, but the life that he so patiently led.

The following are two passages of Scriptures to help improve your ministry focus:

"THEREFORE SEEING we have this ministry, as we have received mercy, we faint not; But have renounced the hidden things of dishonesty, not walking in craftiness, nor handling the word of God deceitfully; but by manifestation of the truth commending ourselves to every man's conscience in the sight of God. But if our gospel be hid, it is hid to them that are lost. In whom the god of this world hath blinded the minds of them which believe not, lest the light of the glorious gospel of Christ, Who is the image of God, should shine unto them. For we preach not ourselves, but Christ Jesus the Lord; and ourselves your servants for Jesus' sake. For God, Who commanded the light to shine out of darkness, hath shined in our hearts, to give the light of the knowledge of the glory of God in the face of Jesus Christ."   —2 Corinthians 4:1–6

"WE THEN, as workers together with him, beseech you also that ye receive not the grace of God in vain. (For he saith, I have heard thee in a time accepted, and in the day of salvation have I succoured thee: behold, now is the accepted time; behold, now is the day of salvation.) Giving no offence in any thing, that the ministry be not blamed: but in all things approving ourselves as the ministers of God, in much patience, in afflictions, in necessities, in distresses, in stripes, in imprisonments, in tumults, in labours, in watchings, in fastings; by pureness, by knowledge, by longsuffering, by kindness, by the Holy Ghost, by love unfeigned. By the word of truth, by the power of God, by the armour of righteousness on the right hand and on the left, by honour and dishonour, by evil report and good report: as deceivers, and yet true: as unknown, and yet well known; as dying, and, behold, we live; as chastened, and not killed; as sorrowful, yet always rejoicing; as poor, yet making many rich; as having nothing, and yet possessing all things. O ye Corinthians, our mouth is open unto you, our heart is enlarged."* —2 Corinthians 6:1–11*

Read Matthew 25:14–30 for an excellent story about servants and the talents their lord had given them. Think about the way they used their gifts, whether they multiplied them or hid them.

Suggested Resources . . .

Books:
Daughters of Destiny, compiled and edited by Noelle Wheeler Goforth
Mary Jones and Her Bible, by M.E.R.

CDs:
What's a Girl to Do? by Douglas Phillips
Victory for Daughters, by Kelly Brown, Sarah, Rebekah, & Hannah Zes

---

An Extra Thought . . .
God's Design for Ministry for Young Women

This week, I listened to a wonderful CD set titled "Victory for Daughters" by Kelly Brown, Sarah, Rebekah, and Hannah Zes. The four speakers were formerly home educated, and are now in their twenties. They spoke out about "virtue, serving their fathers, and the noble call of womanhood." It was very convicting. I realized that this past year my desires have been at times selfish, and I have not always spent time with the Lord as I should. I was also encouraged to press on in godly living and to humbly and quietly serve the Lord by ministering in my home. Let me share with you something really neat that Kelly Brown pointed out.

Kelly said that often girls are distracted from the design God has set up for their ministries. Instead of embracing God's design for ministry, many women and girls are seeking their ministry and job outside of the home. We ought to be cautious! The Bible says that women are to be "keepers at home . . . that the Word of God be not blasphemed." (See Titus 2.) As Kelly approached her senior graduation, she was asked a lot of questions like, "What are you going to do with your life?" or "What are you going to do for a ministry?"

Being a wise daughter, Kelly went to the Word of God to define the ministry, job, and role of a woman. Here is what she found:

Women are called to be **helpers.** *"And the LORD God said, It is not good that the man should be alone; I will make him an help meet for him."*

—*Genesis 2:18* One day, you will likely be a helper to your own family. For right now, however, you have a perfect opportunity to be a helper to your father and mother, brothers and sisters. Use this time to prepare for the future!

Women are called to be **homemakers**. *"To be discreet, chaste, keepers at home, good, obedient to their own husbands, that the word of God be not blasphemed."*—*Titus 2:5* We need to learn now the homemaking skills, as well as the practical ways to keep a house. The best way to do this is to help our moms! ☺ We also need to learn to obey our parents. We girls will be under authority the rest of our lives, and now is the best time to practice honoring, respecting, and submitting to the will of our father and mother.

Women are called to be **trainers and teachers**. *". . . bring them up in the nurture and admonition of the Lord."*—*Ephesians 6:4* Do we realize that we may be responsible for raising some of the next generation of Christians? Begin reading and *studying* God's Word *now*. In order to be a teacher, you must first be a student. Start soaking your mind in the Scriptures now!

Women are called to be **a demonstration of unfading beauty**. *"But let it be the hidden man of the heart, in that which is not corruptible, even the ornament of a meek and quiet spirit, which is in the sight of God of great price."*—*1 Peter 3:4*. A content woman, though she may not be outwardly "attractive," is much more beautiful than a woman who does not have the meek and quiet spirit yet possesses the latest style of every clothing, makeup, and jewelry. We need to realize that true joy and contentment comes in Christ, and Christ alone. Nothing else can make us unceasingly happy.

Women are called to be **domestic entrepreneurs**. *Proverbs 31.* Read the Proverbs 31 passage, and you will see that the virtuous woman's ministry begins with her home. The other things fall under this first calling. While it is not wrong to participate in outside ministries, we do need to be cautious that we are truly honoring God and fulfilling His design and will for our lives in ministry.

Many girls spend their teenage years pursuing self-interests. However, I agree with Kelly: life is too short for that. We need to focus on Christ, and make "knowing Him" our primary goal in this season of our lives. It may be sooner than you think that you are trying to run a house on your own—will you be prepared for it? Now is the time to focus on Jesus Christ, and now is the time to prepare for tomorrow. *"There is difference also between a wife and a virgin. The unmarried woman careth for the things of the Lord, that she may be holy both in body and in spirit: but she that is married careth for the things of the world, how she may please her husband."*—1 Corinthians 7:34 Are we going to be some of the "people" included in Nate Saint's challenge, "People . . . are expending their lives . . . and when the bubble has burst they will have nothing of eternal significance to show for the years they have wasted."

I'll have to admit that lately I have found myself seeking selfish desires. But I am now convinced that life is passing too quickly for me to spend these free years doing things for myself. I need to use them to prepare for the future, and to work on my ministry of serving in the home. Please think about this when you are offered ministry opportunities. Just because it is a good thing doesn't make it God's plan for your life. He may desire you to stay in the home, and learn to work behind the scenes as a helper does.

Do you ever go through a day, and all you do is school, chores, help, and daily things like that? When I have a day that doesn't seem to include time for just me to work on my personal business (☺), I sometimes go to bed thinking "I got nothing done today. What a waste." This is very foolish thinking! I need to realize that my personal business is not my goal. My goal is Jesus Christ—serving Him. And serving Him is serving my family right here inside our own four walls. Nothing could be greater, or more desired. That is God's plan, and that is what works. Praise the Lord!

"Let no man despise thy youth; but be thou an example of the believers, in word, in conversation, in charity, in spirit, in faith, in purity. Till I come, give attendance to reading, to exhortation, to doctrine."—1 Timothy 4:12–13 Press on and seek the Lord in all you do!

Application...

"And be ye doers of the word, and not hearers only, deceiving your own selves."—James 1:22

Do you feel that you have "purpose" in life? What is that ultimate purpose? _____
_____
_____

What gifts has God given you? How can you use them for His glory?
_____
_____

In what specific ways can God use you to glorify Him? _____
_____

List two Scriptures that suggest we should glorify Christ: _____
_____

Choose one of the following Scriptures to memorize and recite:

2 Corinthians 4:1–6   *1 Corinthians 10:31*
2 Corinthians 3:2–3   *Matthew 5:13–16*

Recited to: _____ Date: _____

Choose one of the following activities to work on:

- Does you family have a ministry? If not, talk to your parents about starting a family ministry that you could help them in. Seek the Lord for counsel.

- Pray about a small ministry that God could use you in. Talk to your parents, and consider something that would encourage others to grow in the Lord.

–Chapter IV–
Becoming a Daughter of Delight

"My son, despise not the chastening of the LORD; neither be weary of his correction: for whom the LORD loveth he correcteth; even as a father the son in whom he delighteth."
—*Proverbs 3:11–12*

Honoring My Parents and their Authority As a Blessing from God

Carolyn sighed. "Why is it that every time Mom or Dad say 'no' I get so upset? Why can we not have a decent relationship where I trust them? I want to, but I know that in truth, I am not appreciative of their authority."

Every girl should learn to appreciate her parents' authority. It is a blessing! How does she view it that way?

A Daughter of Delight

"Hearken unto thy father that begat thee, and despise not thy mother when she is old. Buy the truth, and sell it not; also wisdom, and instruction, and understanding. The father of the righteous shall greatly rejoice: and he that begetteth a wise child shall have joy of him. Thy father and thy mother shall be glad, and she that bare thee shall rejoice. My son, give me thine heart, and let thine eyes observe my ways." —Proverbs 23:22–26

Parents have a love for their children that the children cannot understand until they have children of their own. Very often, tension rises between parents and daughters because of miscommunication or a lack of understanding. Parents do not understand why their daughters do not trust them, and daughters fail to see why their parents make the choices they do. This can cause hurt feelings and a miserable relationship instead of the beautiful one it could be.

Every parent desires to have a daughter that they can delight in, and this takes much effort on the girl's part. She must show a trusting spirit and a loving heart. A girl's parents should be her heroes and role models, but we must admit that parents and children sin. So what should we do about it? Instead of worrying about the mistakes they sometimes make, we should look past the negative and see the positive. (An example of this is about Noah and his sons; see Genesis 9:20–27.) This will create in the daughter a love and admiration for her parents and in the parents a delight in their daughter.

Strive with all your heart to honor your parents and become a daughter in whom they are well-pleased and delight in. This will not only strengthen your relationship with them now, but how it will benefit your future! I have some friends whose parents are merely their mother and father; other friends have made their parents everything to them. That is evident by their warm hugs and desire to be around their parents. They know that in their parents they can find the love, strength, and comfort that only a parent can give. They have given to their parents their heart, and, in exchange, the parents trust their daughter and delight in her.

Earnestly strive to make your parents your best friends! Let them delight in you by your reverence for them, your longing to be with and like them, and your ability to look past their weaknesses, only seeing their strengths. Be a daughter in whom your parents can truly delight, trust, love, and appreciate.

> *"A good daughter* is the steady light of her parent's house. Her father's memory is forever connected with that of his happy fireside. She is his morning sunlight—his evening star."
>
> —from *Daughters of Destiny*

Do They Trust in You?

In Proverbs 31, we have the outline of a virtuous woman. Many of the qualities we see in her are things to do with her husband trusting her. This is great to apply today, even as daughters, because we can replace "husband" with "parents." Think of the happy man you will make one day by practicing now to love the authority God has placed in your life! ☺

"Who can find a virtuous woman? for her price is far above rubies. The heart of her husband doth safely trust in her, so that he shall have no need of spoil. She will do him good and not evil all the days of her life."—Proverbs 31:10–12

Do your parents trust in you? Do they know that you will take initiative to do the thing that is right when facing temptation, or that you will complete a task that needs to be done? Are they confident that you speak well of them to your friends? Do they trust that you will obey them and do what they ask even if they are not around? A daughter who can be trusted is a daughter to delight in.

This is one of the qualities of a virtuous woman. *"A virtuous woman is a crown to her husband: but she that maketh ashamed is as rottenness in his* bones."—*Proverbs 12:4* Are you a crown to your parents? If so, you will one day be a crown to your future husband. Or do you, on the other hand, bring so much shame that it is as if their bones were rotting? *"A wise son maketh a glad father: but a foolish son is the heaviness of his mother."* —*Proverbs 10:1*

Let me also encourage you—never hide anything from your mother. A girl who is open with her mother and makes her mother her best friend and confident will prosper much more quickly than a girl who keeps secrets from her mother and avoids the relationship. You must be open with your mother! You must communicate!

No Secrets

"The moment a girl has a secret from her mother, or has received a letter she dare not let her mother read, or has a friend that her mother does not know, she is in danger. A secret is not a good thing for a girl to have. The fewer secrets that lie in the hearts of women at any age, the better. It is almost a test of purity. She who has none of her own is best and happiest. In girlhood hide nothing from your mother. The girl who frankly says to her mother, 'I have been there; met so and so; such and such remarks were made, and this or that was done,' will be sure of receiving good advice and sympathy. If all was right no fault will be found. If the mother knows, out of her great experience, that something was improper or unsuitable, she will, if she is a good mother, kindly advise against its repetition. You may not know, girls, just what is right—just what is wrong, yet. You can't be blamed for making little mistakes; but you will never do anything very wrong if from the first you have no secrets from your mother."

—from *Verses of Virtue*

Dedicated Daughter

In the book of Ruth, we find that this woman was truly dedicated to her mother-in-law. Her husband had died, and she said she would follow her husband's mother wherever she went.

Chapter Four—Becoming a Daughter of Delight

"And Ruth said, Entreat me not to leave thee, or to return from following after thee: for whither thou goest, I will go; and where thou lodgest, I will lodge: thy people shall be my people, and thy God my God: Where thou diest, will I die, and there will I be buried: the LORD do so to me, and more also, if aught but death part thee and me." —Ruth 1:16–17

Are we daughters of dedication to our parents? When they ask us to do something, are we quick to respond, "Yes, I would be glad to"? Do we follow them in whatever path they choose?

Parents must make decisions. Sometimes the daughter is not happy about the decision her parents have made (change of churches, moving, a new schedule, etc.). Though she has no choice but to comply, her heart is not with her parents. A dedicated daughter, however, will willingly and cheerfully serve alongside her parents and work with them to complete their goal. This virtuous daughter will become a delight to her parents.

When I think of a dedicated daughter, a very pleasant woman, Noelle Wheeler Goforth, comes to mind. Although I do not know her personally, I was encouraged by listening to her father, Richard "Little Bear" Wheeler, speak of her courtship testimony.

Mr. Wheeler talked about Noelle's earliest years. Even as a young child, she was dedicated to her father, and submitted to his plans and desire for her life. There were many times when she wanted to do something that her father was hesitant about, yet she willingly accepted his authority.

In her teen years, Noelle diligently served her father in his ministry, *Mantle Ministries*. She trusted him with her heart, and promised to submit to his counsel about her future life partner. Though she may have been anxious about marriage at times, she knew that God would work through her father to bring the perfect man as her husband.

All through her years as a single girl at home, Noelle demonstrated trust and dedication to her parents. Because of her patience and willing heart, God blessed her with a life partner. Today Noelle lives with her husband and three children in Bulverde, Texas. What an awesome example of a dedicated daughter! *Thank you, Noelle!* ♥

Grace to Your Head

So many girls and women view authority as something that is limiting their freedom and independence. But God knew what He was doing when He placed man over woman. This has been one of the greatest blessings yet.

"My son, hear the instruction of thy father, and forsake not the law of thy mother: For they shall be an ornament of grace unto thy head, and chains about thy neck."—Proverbs 1:8–9

These verses remind us how precious authority is! Do you realize where you might be right now were it not for your parents' blessed authority? Maybe you feel that you should have more control over the decisions in your life, or that you are capable of "fending for yourself" most of the time. Your argument might be that you are too old for someone else to tell you what to do. I have news for you—the rest of your life, you will be under authority. God designed it this way! Single women (before marriage) are under the authority of their parents. Married women are under the authority of their husband. Widows are under the Lord's authority. Learn now to trust and appreciate your parents' authority.

I am not trying to make it sound easy and exciting! ☺ I struggle with submitting to my parents at times too. I have had thoughts like "I'm old enough to . . ." or, "I can make this decision myself" or, "Why can't I do this; most girls my age can?" However, God is teaching me, that *through Him* I can learn the protection and joys of being under authority. I must humble myself and allow Him to work through the efforts of my parents.

How do you start loving authority that limits you? I believe the answer is trusting in God to work through your parents. If you will trust Him, you will learn to trust your parents. Give up everything—your desires, goals, plans, your life—first to God, and second to your parents. This trust in your parents starts with a yielding of your life to the Heavenly Father.

"Lord, I give up all my own purposes and plans, all my own desires and hopes and ambitions, and accept Thy will for my life. I give myself, my life, my all utterly to Thee, to be Thine forever. I hand over to Thy keeping all my friendships; all the people whom I love are to take a second place in my heart. Fill me and seal me with Thy Holy Spirit. Work out Thy whole will in my life, at any cost, now and forever."
—Elizabeth "Betty" Stam

For me, trusting my parents' authority has been difficult at times. Either I fail to see the reward of their guarding me, or I do not agree with what they want to do. I can recall when I was about twelve years old, my longing to attend a certain seminar that discussed Biblical principles for Christian living. My parents had attended it, and they were very blessed and encouraged by the godly insights shared therein. The recommended age was twelve or thirteen and up.

I was just certain I would be an attendee soon, because I knew everything preached was sound, Biblical doctrine. However, when I asked my parents about it, they felt I was too young. They told me that they were not ready for me to be exposed to some of the issues discussed.

For months, even years, I struggled with this in my heart. I was almost to the point of embarrassment when many of my friends had attended. Why? At that time in my life, it simply did not seem fair. I doubted my parents' authority, especially in this area.

Finally I began to pray about the whole thing and asked the Lord to help me accept my parents' authority as a gift from God, and to learn to trust them. He taught me what it meant to give something up to Him, and trust Him to deal with it. When I had truly let go of *all* my desire to do something my parents disapproved of, I was very happy, and it did not bother me at all that I was not allowed to attend the seminar. I decided to trust my parents and not discuss the issue with them anymore. It was no longer a struggle for me.

Still today, I have to trust them in little matters like this. *What is hard for most girls is to trust their parents in the decisions they make that put them in a different position than their friends!* I trust my parents' decision to not "play the dating game," but that is somewhat easy since most of my friends are committed to trusting their parents with their hearts as well. The harder things are what my friends *can* do, or I feel I should be old enough to do. However, by trusting my parents with all those decisions, I am delighting them, and benefiting myself as well. It is such a blessing to trust your parents' loving authority!

Sisters, do you trust your parents' authority? When they ask you not to do something—even if it is a "good" thing—do you accept their will as your own and gladly appreciate their say in things? What about when your parents ask you to do something you do not want to do? Do you do it happily and willingly? Or do you shirk from your task?

I remember when I was little that arrangements were made for me to spend a couple of days at a friend's house. In her subdivision was a public pool, and it was mid-summer! This sounded like fun, but my parents had requested I not swim since they were not going to be there, and I was a little rusty in swimming techniques! ☺

At my age, the "no" to an opportunity was a slight embarrassment, and though my friend's mom knew I could not swim, I was hoping my friend would not ask about it. No sooner had I walked in the door and settled all my belongings into her room, when she asked, "We're going swimming, right? Did you bring your swim suit?"

She evidently did not know I was restricted from this activity. I hesitantly explained that I was not allowed to. Her response was quite a surprise to me, "Oh that is so wonderful your parents love you so much! I wish my parents cared for me as your parents do! And I wish they would home school me like your parents home school you!"

Although I marveled at this, it helped me to appreciate my parents more. Parents who exercise loving authority are a rare blessing, especially when the children are grateful for it. Thank God for your parents and for their desire to keep you out of harm's way! They are protecting you, and you should *appreciate* their authority. The Bible says that *"the earth is disquieted and cannot bear" "an odious woman when she is married; and an handmaid that is heir to her mistress."—Proverbs 30: 21, 23*

While this may take some patience, the Lord will help you to give up your desires to Him. When you give your life to the Lord, asking Him to take care of it, you do not have to be afraid. Soon you will be able to trust the Lord and your parents because you know it all rests in the hands of God Who knows more than even our parents can ever know.

> "Thou wilt keep him in perfect peace, whose mind is stayed on thee: because he trusteth in thee. Trust ye in the LORD for ever: for in the LORD JEHOVAH is everlasting strength." —Isaiah 26:3–4

> "For My thoughts are not your thoughts, neither are your ways My ways, saith the LORD. For as the heavens are higher than the earth, so are My ways higher than your ways, and My thoughts than your thoughts."—Isaiah 55:8–9

> "LIKEWISE, YE WIVES, be in subjection to your own husbands; that, if any obey not the word, they also may without the word be won by the conversation of the wives; while they behold your chaste conversation coupled with fear. Whose adorning let it not be that outward adorning of plaiting the hair, and of wearing of gold, or of putting on of apparel; but let it be the hidden man of the heart, in that which is not corruptible, even the ornament of a meek and quiet spirit, which is in the sight of God of great price. For after this manner in the old time the holy women also, who trusted in God, adorned themselves, being in subjection unto their own husbands: even as Sarah obeyed Abraham, calling him lord: whose daughters ye are, as long as ye do well, and are not afraid with any amazement." —1 Peter 3:1–6

A daughter is truly beautiful because of her submissive spirit. You might remember Sarah, in the Old Testament, who was acknowledged for her willingness to submit to and trust her husband. We find through reading God's Word that her husband lied about her being his wife, because she was so beautiful. Can you imagine? Her godly submission brought beauty to her countenance. (Read Genesis 12 and 20.) Additionally, we are told in Proverbs 1:8–9 that submitting to authority adds beauty not just to our lives, but is like beauty to our bodies as well. It is unfading beauty.

> *"Next to your duty to God* comes your duty to your parents; and you can never form an excellent, amiable, and lovely character, unless the foundation of it is laid in filial piety, as well as

in piety towards God. Solomon says to the young, 'Hear the instruction of thy father, and forsake not the law of thy mother; for they shall be an ornament of grace unto thy head, and chains about thy neck.' Nothing will make you appear so lovely in the eyes of others as a dutiful behavior towards your parents; and nothing will make you appear so unamiable and unlovely as a disrespectful, disobedient carriage towards them. No ornament sits so gracefully upon youth as filial piety; no outward adorning can compare with it."

—Harvey Newcomb, in *How To Be A Lady*

A girl who rests in peace under her parents' protection of authority will be content in her life, and will be happy with the choices her parents make. Her life will be truly beautiful because she is trusting in her parents, therefore, trusting in the Lord. Remember that the heart of your parents is in the hand of the Lord. (See Proverbs 21:1.) A daughter who trusts her parents' authority, and follows it, will be a beautiful delight to her parents, a crown to adorn their heads and lives. *"Whose adorning let it not be that outward adorning . . . But let it be the hidden man of the heart, . . . even the ornament of a meek and quiet spirit, which is in the sight of God of great price."*—1 Peter 3:3–4

"*Why submission works* is a mystery. Every mature woman who embraces it is amazed to find out that there are layers and layers of it to experience still. But with the giving up of one's rights, ways, and even wishes comes the gaining of an ageless beauty secret. Just look around you. Note the women who have it and the women who don't. Where does real beauty reside? Cosmetics cover up. Godliness shows up. It gives up the inner beauty to register upon the face."

—Renee Ellison, in *Sarah's Beauty Secret*

Obedience & Honor

"Children, obey your parents in the Lord: for this is right. Honour thy father and mother; which is the first commandment with promise; that it may be well with thee, and thou mayest live long on the earth."—Ephesians 6:1–3

A daughter who obeys her parents is a delight. All throughout Scripture (specifically the Proverbs), we see that parents are to instruct their children in righteousness. The children are to obey willingly and cheerfully, and they are to honor their parents with a special reverence. Just as in Noelle's experience, by honoring and obeying her father when she was a child, this prepared her for marriage and for honoring and obeying her husband.

It is more and more common today for children to disrespect their parents. This is sad and confusing. Why do children fail to honor their parents in this day? Regardless of which way the world is going, however, children (and adults) are called to honor their parents in a special way.

One form of honor is facial expressions and words of respect. I have seen children highly disrespect their parents by either their angry looks or harsh words. Have you ever rolled your eyes at your parents? Maybe you have "talked under your breath"? These things are dishonoring! *"The eye that mocketh at his father, and despiseth to obey his mother, the ravens of the valley shall pick it out, and the young eagles shall eat it."* –Proverbs 30:17 God calls every young person to show reverence to her parents because of the position of authority God gave them, and she should be quick to love them. *"Thou shalt rise up before the hoary head, and honour the face of the old man, and fear thy God: I am the LORD."*—Leviticus 19:32

"Do you ask, 'How shall I honor my parents?' In the first place, you must honor them in your heart, by loving and reverencing them, and by cultivating a submissive, obedient disposition. It is not honoring your parents, to indulge an unsubmissive, turbulent spirit. To be angry with your parents, and to feel that their lawful commands are hard or unreasonable, is dishonoring them. The authority which God has given your parents over you is for your good, that they may re-

> strain you from evil and hurtful practices, and require you to do what will be, in the end, for your benefit. When they restrain you, or require you to do what is not pleasing to you, they have a regard to your best interests. To be impatient of restraint, and to indulge hard feelings toward them, is doing them great dishonor. If you could read the hearts of your parents, and see what a struggle it costs them to interfere with your inclinations, you would feel differently. But these rebellious feelings of yours are not only against your parents, but against God, who gave them this authority over you."
>
> —Harvey Newcomb, *How To Be A Lady*

When I was eleven, I met a young lady a few years older than me named Ruth. (☺—the name goes well!) She was a mighty influence on my life to love and honor my parents. I was encouraged by her actions of love to her parents, which is not always quite as evident in other young people.

Ruth showed love to her parents by her affection and kind words of love to or about them. She never gossiped about them or spoke badly of them. She always respected them in her words and facial expressions. She trusted them, loved them, and they were among her best friends. She enjoyed being around them, and desired to be like them.

As a result, Ruth's parents delighted in her. They often spoke of her kindness, and she was known for being a delightful, serving daughter to her parents. What an example of a girl who loves and appreciates her parents and their authority! She trusts them, and thanks God for them. Ruth will never know how much her actions and attitude encouraged and influenced me to do the same for my parents.

Thank you, Ruth, for your godly example of a virtuous daughter, in whom her parents delight! ♥

Rebellion is as Witchcraft

> *"For rebellion is as witchcraft, and stubbornness is as iniquity and idolatry . . ."*
> —1 Samuel 15:23

This verse speaks volumes about the sin of rebellion! It should be a large red flag to never show disrespect or stubbornness to our parents but to always be in obedience to them. It is a serious thing to be a rebellious child, and I hope that no Christian girl allows rebellion to even creep in her heart.

Someone who rebels against her authority is one who refuses to do what she is asked. It can also be a heart attitude. There are times when, outwardly, we may be obedient, but in the heart we may be rebellious. All through the Bible (particularly the Old Testament), we see lives of people who rebelled against God, and God does not tolerate it.

Girls, the worst thing you can do to displease your parents and make yourself a daughter of despair is to rebel against them. Do not even associate with young people who lead rebellious lives. God does not bless the disobedient. A girl who despises her parents' authority is headed for a miserable future.

Remember that as you obey and honor your parents, you are actually obeying and honoring God. Do it in His name and to His glory. Love and respect your parents, and make them your best friends!

"Filial piety adds a peculiar charm to *the female character; while the want of it, in females, makes them appear like monsters. Disobedience, or the want of proper respect and reverence to parents, is so contrary to the gentle nature of your sex, that it makes them appear very unlovely. This defect needs but to be seen, in a girl or a young lady, to spoil all her attractions. No matter how beautiful she is—this defect will be a black spot on her pretty face . . . no matter how genteel she may be in behavior to others—the first step in gentility is, respectful and obedient carriage toward parents. True gentility comes from gentleness of heart; but there can be no gentleness in that female heart which dishonors her parents. No matter with how much elegance and taste she may decorate her beautiful form—this defect will make her appear worse than the most deformed person, clad in tattered garments made up of dirty old shreds and patches. Nor will it be confined to childhood and youth;—there is, perhaps, nothing that has a more important bearing upon the future*

character of children and youth than their treatment of their parents . . . a quick perception of propriety, in regard to the respect due to parents; with a constant watchfulness to show attention, and to anticipate their wants, will adorn a young lady, in the view of all beholders, more than all the finery, and jewels, and other ornaments, that can be heaped upon her. It will make her appear more beautiful than the finest form that was ever beheld, or the most comely countenance that was ever reflected in a mirror."   —Harvey Newcomb, *How To Be A Lady*

Suggested Resources . . .

Books:
The Courtship of Sarah McLean, by Mr. and Mrs. Stephen Castleberry (note: this book is not a "romance novel"! It is a beautiful story of a godly Christian woman who demonstrates trusting submission in the Lord and her parents. Through her "waiting on the Lord" and contentment, God brings her a husband. Excellent to read as a family!)
Dear Princess, by Mary M. Landis (available from: Rod and Staff, Ph. 606-522-4348)

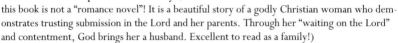

An Extra Thought . . .

The Best Gift You Can Ever Give Your Parents

From *Virtuous Daughters,* By Mrs. Cheryl Schlichter
Note: This article was written around Christmas, therefore it has a Christmas focus.

Christmas is a time when many people give a gift to someone. Do you ever think about your parents' gift and think, "What am I going to give *them* . . . they have everything already!" Well, I know of the *very best* gift you could ever give them. And some more good news . . . it doesn't matter what your budget is . . . you can afford it, because it doesn't cost a dime. That gift is you!

The Bible says that you are a gift from God given to your parents. Let's look at some verses. *"Lo, children are an heritage of the Lord and the fruit of the womb is his reward. As arrows are in the hand of a mighty man; so are children of the youth. Happy is the man that hath his quiver full of them: they shall not be ashamed, but they shall speak with the enemies in the gate."* —Psalm 127:3–5

You are a blessing from God. *"Thy wife shall be as a fruitful vine by the sides of thine house: thy children like olive plants round about thy table. Behold, that thus shall the man be blessed that feareth the Lord."* —Psalm 128:3–4

Also, it doesn't matter if you are an only child, or the first born, second, third, fourth, fifth, or tenth! You are special to God and your parents because you are uniquely you! (Read Psalm 139.)

So, now that we have established that the Bible calls you a gift, and that you are a special gift no matter where your place is in the family, let's talk about how you can daily live out the gift you are.

Purpose this Christmas (and every day) to give your parents...

A HEART that loves and trusts them. I begin with your heart, because a heart that loves and trusts her parents will much easier do all the other things I will mention. It is a heart that is pliable, not rigid. It is a heart that is selfless, not selfish. *"My son, give me thine heart..."* —*Proverbs 23:26* You might be thinking . . . but my parents make mistakes; can I trust them when I think they are making a mistake? Yes, they can make a mistake, but does God make mistakes? Absolutely not! And He has placed your parents over you to love and trust. *"Trust in the Lord with all thine heart and lean not unto thine own understanding. In all thy ways acknowledge Him and He shall direct thy path."*—*Proverbs 3:5–6* If you trust the Lord, you can trust your parents in knowing that the Lord will work through them for your good. *"The Lord wsill perfect that which concerneth me . . ."*—*Psalm 138:8* *"And we know that all things work together for good to them that love God, to them who are the called according to His purpose."*—*Romans 8:28* Furthermore, a girl who loves and trusts her parents (by loving and trusting the Lord) will have a great peace. *"Thou wilt keep him in perfect peace, whose mind is stayed on Thee: because he trusteth in Thee."*—*Isaiah 26:3* So, darling virtuous daughters, give your parents your heart.

A HAND that serves them. Can you give the gift of your hands to your parents? How can you help them? The Proverbs 31 woman used her hands to serve her family. *"she reacheth forth her hands to the needy."*—*Proverbs 31:20* Does your mother or father need something? Perhaps a spill cleaned up, or a glass of water, or what about a soft hug? Consider this verse, *"Be ye strong therefore, and let not your hands be weak: for your work shall be rewarded."*—*2 Chronicles 15:7* So, girls, would you give your parents your hands?

And EYES that honor them. Do you honor your parents with your eyes? Did you know that your eyes tell your parents where your heart is? You might be obeying with your actions, but your eyes reveal your true obedience. They are the windows to what is inside of you. Do you ever roll your eyes at you parents? I hope not. This is a form of disrespect and dishonor. Look at *Proverbs 30:17*: *"The eye that mocketh at his father, and despiseth to obey his mother, the ravens of the valley shall pick it out, and the young eagles shall eat it."* The Bible is clear that this is not acceptable. Can you purpose to give your parents eyes that honor them?

And FEET that are quick to obey them. Do your feet come quickly when called? Do your feet go quickly to bed when told? How quickly your feet respond to obedience is another indication of your heart. Purpose to have feet that obey quickly. Furthermore, have feet that run from evil. *"My son, if sinners entice thee, consent thou not. My son, walk not thou in the way with them; refrain thy foot from their path."*—*Proverbs 1:10,15* Also, consider these verses: *"He that walketh with wise men shall be wise: but a companion of fools shall be destroyed."*—*Proverbs 13:20* *"The eyes of the Lord are in every place, beholding the evil and the good."* —*Proverbs 15:3* So, dear girls, give your parents feet that are quick to obey them and quick to run from evil.

And EARS that listen to their instruction. Do your ears listen to and heed their instruction? Or do you sometimes "tune out" when they are talking to you? There are many wonderful verses on this:

Proverbs 1:8	*Proverbs 4:1*	*Proverbs 13:1*
Proverbs 2:2,5	*Proverbs 4:10*	*Proverbs 15:5*

So, darling virtuous daughters, give them the gift of ears that listen to their instruction.

A MIND that appreciates them. Do you think grateful thoughts toward your parents? Do you notice and think about all they do for you? Perhaps you can sit down and write ten things that you are grateful for in your parents. Then think about these things when you are with them. You will reflect it in your smile and affection. Don't forget to thank God for your parents, too. *"I thank my God upon every remembrance of you."*—*Philippians 1:3* Purpose to give them the gift of a mind that appreciates them.

And a MOUTH that respects them. It is so sad to me when I hear a girl's mouth disrespect her father or mother. And the pain that the parent feels is greater still. Please dear virtuous daughters, only speak words of respect to your parents. *"Her children arise up, and call* her blessed . . ."—Proverbs 31:28 *"Pleasant words are as an honecomb, sweet to the soul, and health to the bones."*—Proverbs 16:24 Now consider these verses: *"He that keepeth his mouth keepeth his life: but he that openeth wide his lips shall have destruction."*—Proverbs 13:3 *"Death and life are in the power of the tongue: and they that love it shall eat the fruit thereof."*—Proverbs 18:21 So, please dear girls, won't you give your parents the gift of a mouth that respects them?

Remember, darling daughters, that no gift you could ever buy your parents—even if it cost millions of dollars—could ever be as great as the gift of yourself. But if you are thinking, "I can't do this; it's just too hard!" do not forget that in your own strength it is impossible to do these things, but with God, all things are possible. As you love and trust the Lord, and seek Him, He will mold you little by little, day by day. Don't give up, dear girls! The Lord is faithful, even when we are not. And His forgiveness and mercies are new every morning! As you live a life that is a blessing and a gift to your parents, you will be blessed in return beyond measure. *"Children, obey your parents in the Lord: for this is right. Honour thy father and mother; which is the first commandment with promise; that it may be well with thee, and thou mayest live long on the earth."*—Ephesians 6:1–3

Darling virtuous daughters, I will pray for you as you seek to be a treasured gift to your parents this Christmas, as well as all year long!

Application . . .

"But be ye doers of the word, and not hearers only, deceiving your own selves."—James 1:22

Do you trust and appreciate your parents' authority? If not, look up some Scriptures to help in this area: _____
_____
_____

List two Scriptures that suggest the importance of honoring your parents: _____

Do your parents delight in you? Do they trust in you? Why or why not?
_____
_____
_____

List a daughter from God's Word whose parents delighted in her because she honored and trusted them: _____

Choose one of the following Scriptures to memorize and recite:

1 Peter 3:1–6   Ruth 1:16–18
Proverbs 1:8–9   Proverbs 3:11–12

Recited to: _____ Date: _____

Choose one of the following activities to work on:

- Write a note thanking your parents for their loving authority and give it to them.

- Next time you are with your friends, encourage them in appreciating their parents' loving authority and speak well of your own parents.

–Chapter v–
Becoming a Sister of Love

"Behold, how good and how pleasant it is for brethren to dwell together in unity! It is like the precious ointment upon the head . . . as the dew that descended upon the mountains of Zion: for there the LORD commanded the blessing, even life for evermore."
—Psalm 133:1–3

Loving My Siblings
As Best Friends and Precious Treasures

Dorothy and Louise were two friends who had a lot in common. They both loved the Lord, they both enjoyed cooking and sewing, and they really liked to talk! Nevertheless, one thing was different about the two—Dorothy found unusual confidence, encouragement, and security in her siblings while Louise's relationship with her siblings was distant.

Dorothy constantly talked of her siblings and their accomplishments. She supported her older brother in his college training. She helped her sister learn to sew and cook. She helped her younger brother with school. She loved to be around them and she enjoyed the time she spent with them.

Louise would like a close friendship with her siblings too. However, she knows it is more than just their interests "clicking." She is beginning to realize that being best friends with your siblings is a beautiful thing, but like any other friendship, it takes lots of tender loving care.

Blessings in Disguise

I have heard a sadly large number of girls complain about their siblings. They whine that their sisters are always in the way or that their brothers drive them up the walls. I would like to encourage you, if you have siblings, that they can be your best friends and closest confidents if you work with them to build that relationship.

I am the first born in our quiver ☺, and my four siblings are by far my best friends! Each one is special to me for a different reason, and I love to spend time with them!

Justin is thirteen years old, and is my close companion. We enjoy spending time together, and I enjoy the strong confidence I find in my brother, as he is such a fine young man!

Brittany is eight years old, and she is my sweet sister. We share a room, and like to spend "sister-sister" time. She is a special friend because we can do "girl things" together.

Gideon is five years old, and the cutest little guy! We are "pals" and enjoy doing cross word puzzles together. He also likes me to write silly sentences for him to read.

Ethan is two years old, and my little sweetie. We like to read books together, and he especially likes to ride on my neck, which can be tiring for me ☺, but fun for him to be so high!

Sometimes, siblings really do come as blessings in disguise. Actually, it seems that most every child comes that way. As a child grows, he will get into mischief, and will need assistance. Sometimes parents feel discouraged with their child's behavior. Nevertheless, if they are diligent to work with that child, he will grow up into a fine man or woman of God.

I am aware that many girls who have complained about their siblings really do have naughty siblings. These girls might feel discouraged that their relationship as friends is impossible. Still, the truth is that God gave you your siblings for a special reason, and He longs for you to make them your best friends and to be their best friend. For girls with all young siblings, becoming best friends may be harder, but I think it is definitely an achievable goal for girls with siblings even several years apart.

Better yet, it is not only a goal. It is a thrilling opportunity, adventure, journey, encouragement, and blessing. Making your siblings your best friends will literally change your life, and you will never regret it. There is a special bond in this relationship that can be found in no other. I cannot explain the joy I have found in making my siblings my best friends!

Siblings as Best Friends

I recently overheard a conversation that caught my interest. It was between two teenage girls, and went something like this: (names have been changed)

Sylvia, in a sympathetic tone: "Are you going to miss your brother when he goes away?"

Linda, somewhat carelessly: "Not really. I rarely see him anyway."

Later, the girl whose brother was moving was speaking to another woman who asked how he was doing. Her response, again, was quite careless, "Oh I don't know. I never talk to him when he calls. I guess he's doing fine." She gave as much information as she knew of his work, and that was very little.

This girl was not trying to avoid her brother—I know that. She is one of many children, and they all get along fine. What she has been unconsciously missing, however, is *friendship, close friendship*. I was saddened at this, because her relationship with her brother could be so much firmer. She could be supporting him in his endeavors, well pleased with his successes, and helping him with his work. How much more exciting their relationship would be!

The intimate friendship between siblings is so unique and special. It is one that stands through thick and thin. It is one that holds many disappointments, arguments, and tears, but ends up with excitements, hugs, and laughter. You are writing your life story with your best friend right there beside you. It is one of the most important relationships you will ever have.

For me, this special friendship formed as we got older. And I think that it all began when I had no other friends to look to . . .

I was eight years old when we moved away from the home I had known since I could remember. I was sad as we left behind all my best friends and playmates.

The true loneliness did not come, however, until we had lived in our new home a year or two. There were few girls my age at our church, and there were no children in our neighborhood. The friends I used to play with had gone their own ways and I never saw them. I felt lonely.

Every day, I prayed that God would send me a *best* friend—someone who I could talk about everything with, who lived close, who I went places with all the time, who would spend lots of time with me, etc., etc., etc.—I think all my readers know what kind of friend I was imagining. It seems every young girl dreams of such a friend! ☺

For some reason, however, the Lord did not seem to be sending that person. Why? Instead, He sent a special message from His Word. This is what it said: *"A friend loveth at all times, and a brother is born for adversity."—Proverbs 17:17* For years I had not understood that verse, but as someone explained it in a magazine—God gave us siblings, not to *cause* adversity, but to be there *in times of* adversity. Friends are precious and wonderful at encouraging and loving you, but there is a unique support and confidence that one can only find in a close sibling.

This opened my eyes to a special truth, and I began to see that I had had this special friend all the time. Everything that I had imagined in an outside friend, I soon saw in my siblings. This is when I began making my siblings my *best friends*.

This choice has been a huge blessing in my life that I could never fully explain. Through *everything*, my siblings have been there.

Most friendships—even close ones—only last a number of years. The intimate friendship between siblings, however, lasts a *lifetime*. The secrets that you can share, the love that you can show, the time that you can spend together—it is all so different from that of an outside friend.

Outside friendships are beautiful, and it is good for every young girl to have godly chums whom she can spend time with, relate to, and learn from. However, I have come to the realization over the years that few of my friends have really stayed with me forever. Many of them have moved and we have lost touch, regardless of how close we might have been at some point.

Other times I have been disappointed because the more I came to know a friend the more I realized how different we really were. There were times when my feelings were hurt because I felt like a close friend was becoming less of a friend by and by.

Yet, none of these things have bothered me nearly as much as they could. Why? Because my siblings are my closest and most faithful friends. I guess this is best summed up in part of a letter I wrote:

> *"God taught me* to make Him my first best Friend, and my siblings and parents my closest confidents after that. What a blessing this has been to me! For three or four years now I have kept this principle in practice, and to be quite honest, I rarely struggle with loneliness any more. I also have an easier time making friends because I do not have high expectations of their lives or of what our relationship could become."

Built on the Lord

"Except the LORD build the house, they labour in vain that build it: except the LORD keep the city, the watchman waketh but in vain. It is vain for you to rise up early, to sit up late, to eat the bread of sorrows: for so He giveth His beloved sleep." —Psalm 127:1–2

Again, we must realize that in our own strength, we are nothing. The friendship between siblings is much stronger when it is built on the Lord. *"Therefore whosoever heareth these sayings of mine, and doeth them, I will liken him unto a wise man, which built his house upon a rock: and the rain descended, and the floods came, and the winds blew, and beat upon that house; and it fell not: for it was founded upon a rock. And every one that heareth these sayings of mine, and doeth them not, shall be likened unto a foolish man, which built his house upon the sand: and the rain descended, and the floods came, and the winds blew, and beat upon that house; and it fell: and great was the fall of it."* —Matthew 7:24–27

The sibling relationship is able to rough the storms that come along if we build it upon the Rock—Jesus Christ. As a family, we have encountered many tough times, but the neat thing is that we have always had each other to lean on, and Christ and His teachings have remained as a strong foundation. I praise God for His mercy toward our family!

However, do not allow the efforts to build your relationship be work of the flesh—it is the *Lord working through us.* We must seek His help to overcome our bad habits and sinful attitudes. Do not be best friends one day and worst enemies the next. ☺ Love each other with the love that is strong no matter what.

You also build your friendship on the Lord when you spend time in His Word together, when you pray together, when you minister to others together, and when you spend time talking about things of God together. A couple of years ago, I really enjoyed going with Justin to rake our elderly neighbor's yard for him. It was a small thing to do, but it was *something*, and we had fun doing it together. Brittany enjoys it when we read God's Word together. I like to tell Gideon Bible stories or teach him verses. Ethan and I enjoy reading Bible stories, too.

My favorite times with my siblings are the times each of us are "in line with" God's Word. We are happy and joyful, filled with the love of Jesus! Sibling relationships are so fulfilling when built on Jesus!

The Golden Rule

"Therefore all things whatsoever ye would that men should do to you, do ye even so to them: for this is the law and the prophets." —Matthew 7:12

For years, this verse has been paraphrased "Do unto others as you would have others do unto you," and has been affectionately dubbed, "The Golden Rule." Sadly, it is not practiced nearly as much as it is preached.

Do you want to see your relationship with your siblings grow? Show them love and sacrifice by giving of your time and energy. Put them first. Occasionally play a game your brother likes just because he wants you to! Take time to help your sister learn cross stitch. Watch your brother play with cars, and even surprise him by saying that you will play with him. I know you will have more fun than you anticipated! ☺

"Give, and it shall be given unto you; good measure, pressed down, and shaken together, and running over, shall men give into your bosom. For with the same measure that ye mete withal shall it be measure to you again."—Luke 6:38

The key here is to take the focus off what your siblings can do for you but what you can do for them. Several years ago, I was struggling with this very principle. I was expecting one of my siblings to treat me certain ways, and be loving and nice to me in everything they did. Yet God taught me that I needed to shift my focus and learn to love my siblings for who they are, and find out what I could do for them. This brought me closer to my siblings and really strengthened our relationship. I began to delight in doing kind things for them, and it was a real joy! *"A man that hath friends must show himself friendly. . ."*—Proverbs 18:24

"A sister's power over her brother lies in her gentleness and sweetness of temper. If you always show an amiable, sweet, loving disposition, they will love you, and seek to gratify your wishes. But, if you attempt to carry your point by contention, they will shun you, as one who only interferes with their enjoyment."

—Harvey Newcomb, *How To Be A Lady*

Praise vs. Criticism

> *"You are a wonderful helper!" "Did you know that God smiles when you obey me so quickly?" "I am so glad you helped me today; I couldn't have done it without you!" "God is going to bless you for being so diligent and cheerful!"*

> *"PLEASE obey me when I call you!" "Can't you see that I need your help?" "Why don't you work more diligently?" "You are so selfish, and you never do anything for anyone else!"*

After reading the above two paragraphs, which do you prefer that people say to you? Which do you say to others (mainly siblings)?

I have found with my siblings that to praise them in their strengths, rather than criticize them in their weaknesses, is a more effective practice. Mainly with the little ones, to be praised by a big sister means everything! To be criticized by a big sister, on the other hand, means their world just fell apart.

Is it not a common idea that if we tell our siblings they are wrong in something they will realize it and stop? Consequently, that only creates more chaos and leaves discouraged and defeated feelings. However, by praising a sibling in the right, you are encouraging him to go on with what he is doing.

Once when Justin and I were babysitting our three younger siblings, I decided that it would be a nice surprise to clean the house for our parents (only the first born ever thinks of that ☺)! Gideon, who was four at the time, decided that he would be most effective in the kitchen, and I could not resist his help, even though I knew it might not be as much assistance as he anticipated.

Gideon was very motivated and his little hands did as much work as they could do in that big kitchen! His methods were so precious—he used a mini water gun to clean down the table! ☺ I went out of my way to praise his diligence (in front of Justin) and you should have seen his face beam with delight! Had I criticized him for not doing this or that (it always seems easier to find fault than strong points), he would have not been nearly as motivated to clean with us.

Keep in mind the importance of this in everything your siblings do. Praise your sister for getting ready for church on time, your brother for his hard work, and so on. It is also very nice to praise your siblings in front of Mommy and Daddy. ☺

> *"Everyone desires approval*, so when you praise others you make them feel successful. You are elevating their name and reputation and expressing your approval of them. Have you ever realized that you have the power to make someone's day successful, simply by your praise? Also, success breeds more success. That is why a little praise will go so far."
> —Sarah Mally, in *Making Brothers and Sisters Best Friends*

Remember that whatever you praise, you are encouraging in your siblings. If you are praising your sister's outward beauty, you are encouraging her to continue to focus on that. If you praise her inward beauty, she will be more excited to beautify her heart.

These words of encouragement will help anyone to continue in what they are doing right. Often a child does something wrong out of mere desire for attention, so if you give him that attention (even by criticizing him for doing wrong), he might begin to think, "When I do something that Sister doesn't like, she pays attention to me!" Instead, when your sibling does something worthy of praise, give him that praise, and you will likely see a desire in him to continue in that particular quality.

Judge Not

Many siblings struggle with judging one another. Do not let this be a part of your relationship! Instead, love and praise them for their achievements.

> *"Be ye therefore merciful*, as your Father also is merciful. Judge not, and ye shall not be judged: condemn not, and ye shall not be condemned: forgive, and ye shall be forgiven . . . And why beholdest thou the mote that is in thy brother's eye, but perceivest

not the beam that is in thine own eye? Either how canst thou say to thy brother, Brother, let me pull out the mote that is in thine eye, when thou thyself beholdest not the beam that is in thine own eye? Thou hypocrite, cast out first the beam out of thine own eye, and then shalt thou see clearly to pull out the mote that is in thy brother's eye."
—Luke 6:36–37, 41–42

Too often, I have been guilty of this very thing—criticizing my siblings for things, when I myself have been struggling with the same problem, yet I often fail to see *my* faults as easily and quickly. Work at this, not only in the words you speak to your siblings, but also in the thoughts that you think of them.

If you do see a struggle in the life of your sibling, examine your own life, and see what faults you can work on. Then, pray for your sibling, and work on the quality they should be working on in your life as well. You might be surprised how much God works through prayer!

Another area that siblings often struggle in is bringing to remembrance each other's flaws, even if they have already been forgiven. I know there have been times when one of my siblings and I are both angry, and one of us bring up something the other did a long time ago that has already been forgiven. This can cause a lot of ill will and distance in any relationship. "He that covereth a transgression seeketh love; but he that repeateth a matter separateth very friends."—Proverbs 17:9 If you seek a strong and loving relationship with your siblings, you will not bring up their flaws; you will forgive and forget their faults. "Hatred stirreth up strifes: but love covereth all sins."—Proverbs 10:12

A Soft Answer

I could not believe my eyes! Snow! Clean, white, fluffy, beautiful snow—just like in the pictures!

I was thirteen years old, and, being a southern Texan all my life, it was my first time to see snow. Our family was traveling with another family to Colorado in the cold month of January, but we began seeing the snow in New Mexico. Because this was such an amazing sight for my siblings and me, we decided it would be nice to take a rest from driving, and get out of the van to see and play in the snow for just a few minutes.

We stopped at the first rest stop we saw. My siblings and I shuffled out of our seats and buttoned up our coats. We dashed to the foreign blanket of white and broke into a snowball fight. Everybody was having such a fun time!

A woman walked up who worked for the state and kept up the rest stops. I did not notice her until I heard, "Hey, y'all need to stop! You are getting snow on the sidewalks and I have to sweep all this mess up!"

I stopped and looked at her. Inside, I was upset. Could she have some mercy? Although I would never say it, I was thinking of how this was my and all my siblings' first time to see snow, and we were just having a little fun. Is it that big of a deal to sweep the sidewalks, anyway?

Something interrupted my train of rude thoughts. I looked over at my father who walked up to her kindly and with a soft answer, "I'm sorry about the mess, ma'am. Let me sweep it up for you." He took the broom and began sweeping the sidewalk. The woman stood there shocked.

Before I knew what was happening, this formerly grumpy person was talking to us, telling us about the many children she had raised, her life, and the state of New Mexico. Her smile extended from ear to ear, and a passing stranger would have thought we were old friends. When we finally had to leave, she said cheerfully, "Well, y'all come back again! Have a wonderful trip!"

The verse came alive to me. A soft answer had turned away this woman's anger. *"A soft answer turneth away wrath: but grievous words stir up anger."—Proverbs 15:1* There is so much truth to this principle! Though I struggle with giving a "soft answer" at times, I have learned through many experiences, that it is much better to respond kindly to someone who is angry than with words of defense.

God's Word teaches us to "love our enemies." Your siblings are definitely not your enemies, but during disputes, it may seem that way! ☺ Instead of using retaliation, respond with love and kindness. You will be amazed at the surprised look on your sibling's face. *"Wherefore, my beloved brethren, let every man be swift to hear, slow to speak, slow to wrath: for the wrath of man worketh not the righteousness of God."—James 1:19–20*

In hearing of girls' experiences with their angry or selfish siblings, I believe that the key to fixing these problems would be to yield their rights, and give soft answers. Suppose you just sat down peacefully on your bed to read a book, and your brother darts in, snatches the book, and laughs as he runs off with it. (No, my brothers have never done that, but I had to think of an example! ☺) The normal response would be to chase after him, and try to get it back. Do you realize that a soft answer would have a better effect?

Instead of running after your brother and getting into a fight, why not try just smiling, getting off your bed, and finding something else to do. Yield your rights to God, and then you will not be disappointed when things are taken from you. Also, your brother might be surprised when he finds out that he did not take *your* book, but *God's*! ☺

Friends Forever

"Why should not a brother make a confidante of his own sister rather than of any other? Why should not a sister look to her own brother for counsel, for protection, for advice, rather than to any other? Why should not brothers be proud to have their own sisters lean upon their arms? And why should not sisters be proud to look up into the faces of their brothers, and feel secure in the shelter of their manly love?"
—J. R. Miller, in Home-Making

This relationship among siblings is so wonderful—it can be such a blessing in a young person's life. I pray that my siblings are my best friends forever. I want my future children to be best friends with their cousins, and I long for a strong family relationship not only now, but in the future. The best thing I can do is start now to build this relationship. It truly can last a lifetime, but it does take work and love!

Be a friend in whom your siblings can find love, support, and comfort. Allow them to find confidence in you, knowing that you will not go around revealing things they may have shared privately with you. *"A froward man soweth strife: and a whisperer separateth chief friends."*—Proverbs 16:28

Also, never forget to laugh! One of the ingredients that have helped create a healthy and good friendship for me and my siblings is laughter. We love to have fun! *"A merry heart doeth good like a medicine: but a broken spirit drieth the bones."—Proverbs 17:22*

Guide and teach your sisters, love and comfort your brothers; be the best sister you can be as you have an overwhelming love for each of your siblings—your best friends and most precious treasures here on earth.

By putting your siblings and their interests first, you will win their hearts fast. Be the sister that you desire to have, pray for guidance and strength, and the Lord will work through you to bless your relationship. I pray that every girl learns and practices the truth that siblings really are a blessing, and can be the best of friends.

Suggested Resources . . .

Books:
Alone yet not Alone, by Tracy Michelle Leininger
The Fisherman's Daughter, rewritten by Mary Zook
Making Brothers and Sisters Best Friends, by Sarah, Stephen, & Grace Mally
(I *highly* recommend this book! Excellent to read with all your siblings or by yourself!)

Tape:
Pineapple Story Tape Series, by Otto Koning (available from: IBLP, Box One, Oak Brook, IL 60522)

An Extra Thought . . .
Making Your Brother Your Best Friend

Do you desire to have a close relationship with your brother? One that will flourish and grow stronger through each trial? Show him love. One of the biggest keys to making your brother your best friend is to love him. Being the oldest of five children, I often "set the mood," and it can be difficult at times to show love and patience. I can say with confidence, however, that my three wonderful brothers are among my best friends. We enjoy being together and like to do fun things. With each brother, our friendship is special in a different way. For example, Justin and I are more prone to sit and chat, while Gideon prefers to show me his farm setup, and Ethan wants me to read him a book. I cherish each of my brothers and thank God for them.

I would like to give you some pointers that I have learned from the Scriptures on the brother-sister relationship. They are very practical, yet profound proverbs that have helped improve and strengthen my relationship with my brothers.

♥ "Thou hast also given me the shield of thy salvation: and Thy right hand hath holden me up, and Thy gentleness hath made me great."—Psalm 18:35
We start with this verse of gratitude written by David because it reveals to us an important truth: God's gentleness, His meekness, was one of the things that made David the strong man he was. Very often

sisters (including myself! ☹) can have a tendency to be hard on their brothers, because they feel like they ought to be showing them right from wrong, or what they did was not kind, or he needs to learn, etc.

But God gave men a natural desire to lead, and He gave women the place to follow their authority's leading. I am not saying that if you have younger brothers you cannot exercise authority over them. When I baby-sit, I am in authority over all my siblings. But God is strengthening me to be gracious and meek—to be gentle. Let your parents discipline your brothers. While there are right times to rebuke your brothers, you ought to be aware that they are few. Justin and I only strive to "correct" each other on issues when it seems necessary, and it is done in a loving, caring manner. I know that when my brother is already upset with me, or I with him, it is not a good time to share one of his weaknesses with him! ☺ Your brothers will make mistakes, but be gentle with them in every way. (See Luke 6:36–37, 41–42 for more on rebuking a brother.)

♥ *"A soft answer turneth away wrath, but grievous words stir up anger."* —*Proverbs 15:1* This goes along with being gentle. When two siblings are arguing about something, and both are hot, if one of them will give a soft answer ("Okay, you're right. I'm sorry; we won't worry about it anymore.") the dispute soon ceases, and everyone is happy again. Give a soft answer in place of defense next time your brother agitates you. The result is wonderful! *"Hatred stirreth up strifes, but love covereth all sins."*—*Proverbs 10:12*

♥ *"A froward man soweth strife: and a whisperer separateth chief friends."* —*Proverbs 16:28* If you truly love your brother and desire to have a strong friendship with him, you will not gossip about him or speak words of disgrace behind his back. The best of friends can become like enemies if they are stirring up unkind words about each other. *"A brother offended is harder to be won than a strong city: and their contentions are like the bars of a castle."*—*Proverbs 18:19*

♥ *"He that covereth a transgression seeketh love; but he that repeateth a matter separateth very friends."* Proverbs 17:9 Here again we are warned that even close friendship can sadly crumble if love is not practiced. Do you desire and seek love in your relationship with your brother? If so, you will not delight in telling your friends or even talking about his struggles in life. While there may be necessary times to express something wrong your brother did to your parents, do not be a "tattle-tale," or always be bringing things to your parents. Do not even recall mistakes your brother has made to him! Your brother will appreciate you more if you strive to *forgive and forget* his flaws.

♥ *"It is better to dwell in the wilderness, than with a contentious and an angry woman."*—*Proverbs 21:19* No one appreciates nagging, brothers in particular. The Bible does not speak favorably of one who is contentious. *"A continual dropping in a very rainy day and a contentious woman are alike."*—*Proverbs 27:15* Drip, drip, drip! Strive to be a cheerful and loving sister, not one that brings discouragement and irritations. It would not be good if instead of becoming best friends with your brothers, you ended up giving them the desire to spend their days on the roof or in the wilderness. ☺ *"It is better to dwell in the corner of the housetop, than with a brawling woman and in a wide house."*—*Proverbs 25:24*

♥ *"A merry heart doeth good like a medicine: but a broken spirit drieth the bones."*—*Proverbs 17:22* Laughter is one of the best ingredients to a strong and lasting friendship among siblings. Brothers and sisters who are always bickering, arguing, or picking on each other are creating malice and tension. Instead, be happy and cheerful; laugh together! Recently Justin and I were left to make supper because my parents decided to go grocery shopping. We ended up having a hilarious time cooking together! It was so much fun! I can testify by my own experiences that laughter is a wonderful dose of medicine; it almost always takes away my discouragement or stress. Be sure to laugh with your brothers many times every day.

Can your brother lean on you when he is down and be confident in your wise counsel and sincere love? Is your brother among your best friends? If not, begin to form that friendship with him, because it is one of the most beautiful and blessed friendships God will every give you!

The Brother's Confident
—From Daughters of Destiny

A good sister's love always holds a cherished place in the grateful memory of the brother! Many men have found a sister's love their ready and cheering resource. His confidence is set in her counsel and he is satisfied with the assurance that it will be uprightly and considerately given. How intimate is the friendship of such sisters! What a reliance for warning, excitement, and sympathy has each secured in each! How many are the brothers to whom, when thrown into the circumstances of temptation, the thought of a sister's love has been a constant, holy presence, rebuking every wayward thought!

The relation of brothers and sisters forms another important element in the happy influences of home. A boisterous or selfish boy may try to domineer over the weaker or more dependent girl, but generally the latter exerts a softening, sweetening charm. The brother animates and heartens; the sister mollifies, tames, refines. The vinetree and its sustaining elm are the emblems of such a relation—and by such agencies our "sons may become like plants grown up in their youth, and our daughters like cornerstones polished after the similitude of a temple."

Sisters scarcely know the influence they have over their brothers. A young man once testified that the greatest proof to the truth of Christian religion was his sister's life.

The excellent book this excerpt was taken from can be purchased from Mantle Ministries; *see "Godly Resources" for addresses.*

Application...

"But be ye doers of the word, and not hearers only, deceiving your own selves."—James 1:22

Are you and your siblings best friends? If not, what is preventing that blessed relationship? _____
_____
_____

How can you strengthen your relationship with your siblings? List two Scriptures that would encourage you to love your siblings: _____
_____
_____

Whom do you that sets a good example of a godly relationship with his/her siblings? _____ What is it that makes this relationship strong? _____
_____
_____

Choose one of the following Scriptures to memorize and recite:
Proverbs 17:9   Proverbs 15:1
Proverbs 10:12   Luke 6:27– 45

Recited to: _____ Date: _____

Choose one of the following activities to work on:

- Go to a sibling you struggle with "getting along," and clear things up. Then work diligently at loving them by notes of encouragement, prayer, small gifts, and acts of service.

- Pray for your siblings by name, given them a hug, and tell them "I love you," each day.

–Chapter vi–
Becoming a Daughter of Discernment

"He that walketh with wise men shall be wise: but a companion of fools shall be destroyed." —Proverbs 13:20

Choosing Friends Wisely & Being a Friend that Honors God

"I wonder," Elizabeth pondered as she twirled her hair in her hand, "I just wonder if I should spend time with Leslie. She's nice and all, but . . . well, I'm not sure if she's a godly influence in my life."

Elizabeth is wise in discerning whether her friendships are good. Do you think that your relationships with other girls are wholesome and edifying, or are they only leading to foolishness?

God's Special Gifts

We seemed to "click" with the first few visits. In just a short time, we became close friends, and our blossoming friendship grew stronger as we made Jesus Christ our true focus. Even the sudden separation of distance did not hurt our relationship. Phone calls, frequent letters, and treasured, occasional visits continue to strengthen our friendship and our walk with the Lord. I thank God for this special friend, as well as the many others He has blessed me with.

Friendship is no doubt a gift from the Lord. In each friend He gives us, He always includes a special lesson that stays with us forever. Friends bring many joys and memories—adventurous hikes, long talks, wet boat rides, sticky and messy crafts, long but fun camping trips, not-so-successful cooking, and sharing how God has been working in each others' lives. Thank God for your friends, and pray for them each day! *"A friend loveth at all times . . ."—Proverbs 17:17*

Personally, I am grateful for the fellowship and encouragement the Lord provided to me through several godly friends. After a period of loneliness and praying for a friend, He brought into my life several girls who have truly made a difference.

God's gift of friendship is beautiful, because as we go through this life, each day and one step at a time, they come and go to encourage and strengthen us. They support and love us. Friends are a blessing!

"A friendship can weather most things and thrive in thin soil—but it needs a little mulch of letters and phone

calls and small silly presents every so often—just to save it from drying out completely."

—Pam Brown

Using Discernment

"Flee also youthful lusts: but follow righteousness, faith, charity, peace, with them that call on the Lord out of a pure heart." —2 Timothy 2:22

Choosing friends wisely is an issue that must be covered. It is a tragedy when a godly young person falls into the wrong group of friends. The results can be devastating. We have plain warning in the Scriptures to choose our friends wisely; let us *always* heed that admonition.

Although most of my friends have been Christians, I have had friends who "rubbed off" on me, even in little things. When a friend was over for the day, and my mom needed help in the kitchen, if my friend complained, I was very likely to have the same attitude. If a selfish friend spent the day, it seemed that I was selfish the entire next day! On the other hand, I have had godly friends influence me for the good. I remember visiting a friend while she was camping; she set a godly example of a good sister to her siblings, and the next several days I was extra careful how I treated my siblings. We seldom realize the influence our friends can have on us! *"He that walketh with wise men shall be wise: but a companion of fools shall be destroyed."*—Proverbs 13:20

"Be not deceived: evil communications corrupt good manners."—1 Corinthians 15:33 If you think about it, you will notice that the people you spend the most time with are the people you are most like. You can also relate this to books you read, music you listen to, or TV you watch. Children who attend school out of home are often more like their peers than their parents or siblings, because they spend the majority of their time with their friends. *"For as he thinketh in his heart, so is he . . ."*—Proverbs 23:7

Mary Landis said the following in her excellent book, *Dear Princess*:

"A good rule for the princess to follow in choosing her friends is to be friendly to all, but intimate with none. This rule [is] a safeguard. But always share your secret heart of hearts only with

Mother or Father. There you will find the love and wisdom that will nurture and tend with delicate care the lovely plant of young womanhood that is slowly and surely unfolding. Within your heart it unfolds leaf by leaf and petal by petal, until a full-blown rose stands trembling and lovely, waiting for a life of love and usefulness under the tender hand of the Master Gardener, our heavenly King."

If your companions are godly and wise, and your parents approve of your friendship with them, you will be blessed immensely! They will likely influence you for the good, and your friendship will flourish in the Lord.

However, if you sense that some of your friends are careless about their walk with the Lord, and your parents are hesitant about your friendship with them, this is a dangerous situation to continue in. Please do not fall simply because you lacked discernment in choosing wise friends! *"Make no friendship with an angry man; and with a furious man thou shalt not go: lest thou learn his ways, and get a snare to thy soul."* —Proverbs 22:24–25

"Strive not with a man without cause, if he have done thee no harm. Envy thou not the oppressor, and choose none of his ways. For the froward is abomination to the LORD: but His secret is with the righteous."—Proverbs 3:30–32

Sadly, there are a large number of fools in the world today, and many of them are young people. They have believed the selfish motto of the world, "life is short—live for yourself." They lack purpose in life, and simply take each day at a time, living for themselves, and wasting time. Nevertheless, God's Word gives a sure warning against making friends or even spending much time with someone like this.

The second part of this verse reminds us that we should not long to be like those who are sinful. Some girls stay out of the wrong crowd, but their hearts are with the "in group." She does not participate in their foolish activities, but inside she is cheering them on. She will eventually see her own folly.

"He that goeth about as a talebearer revealeth secrets: therefore meddle not with him that flattereth with his lips."—Proverbs 20:19 If you meet a girl who is constantly talking about others and using insincere flattery, it

should be a good indicator to not make friends with her. A girl who compliments in such a "gushy" way simply desires attention and wants others to notice her.

Parents are wonderful counselors as to right and wrong friends. While we are to be kind to and set a good example for everyone, be careful developing close friendships with non-believers or carnal Christians. Be sure that your friends are those who encourage you in God's Word and edify you in your walk with Christ.

Choose friends that strive to honor the Lord in all they do. It has been said that a girl seldom rises higher than the girls she has chosen to be her close friends. If you choose friends that encourage you in your walk with Christ and set a godly example, you will likely want to be like them, and follow their Christian lead. ". . . ever follow that which is good, both among yourselves and to all men."—1 Thessalonians 5:15

Never forget to talk to your parents, and seek their advice and counsel about friendships. They have lived much longer and learned much more—they will help you to see if your friends are helping or hindering your walk with Christ. Parents are excellent counselors in this area! ☺

Some of the wonderful lessons I have learned have been through the influence of a godly friend. Ruth was a role model of a dedicated and delightful daughter who loved her parents with all her heart! Sarah was a few years older than me, and helped keep me focused through a trying time in my life. Stephanie taught me what it means to be a gracious young lady, and how to use words sparingly. Melissa is a constant encouragement to me to follow the Lord in all I do. Brianna is a godly example of a daughter who diligently serves in the home. Hannah is always encouraging me to love and trust God. Emily has been an encouragement in reminding me to laugh! ☺ Many of my friends have had an influence on me for the good. *Thanks to each of you!* ♥

Friendship Evaluation 1:
What My Friends are to Me—

♥ Have my friends ever said, "Don't tell your parents . . ."?

◯ Yes   ◯ No

- ♥ Have my friends ever spoken disrespectfully or rudely of their parents or mine?   ⭘ Yes   ⭘ No
- ♥ Do my friends despise godly authority?   ⭘ Yes   ⭘ No
- ♥ Have my friends ever encouraged me to do something that was wrong?   ⭘ Yes   ⭘ No
- ♥ Have my friends ever gossiped about someone?   ⭘ Yes   ⭘ No
- ♥ Do my friends encourage me in my walk with Christ and in His Word?   ⭘ Yes   ⭘ No
- ♥ Do my friends desire God's best and His perfect will for their lives?   ⭘ Yes   ⭘ No
- ♥ Do my parents approve of and encourage my friendships?   ⭘ Yes   ⭘ No

Fleeing from Evil

I cannot say I have ever had to "flee from evil," but there have been times, especially when I was young, when I had to stand alone in a certain circumstance. I remember several years ago, one of the "fads" among some of my young friends was keeping secrets from their parents. Needless to say, this was a warning that these friends may not be the best to edify me in God's Word. There were times I had to say no to what they wanted me to do. Other times I just had to walk away and then there have been the times that I regret—the times I was not sensitive to the Holy Spirit in resisting temptation when I should have. I have made wrong choices just because I longed for my friends' admiration, or I did not want to sacrifice what was fun for what was right.

Even in the circle of godly young people, you are likely to face a decision—either do what your companion does even though it is wrong, or to stand alone and do what is right. It is clear in Scripture that there is no excuse for sin, no matter what your friends are doing, or no matter how much fun the sin may seem for the moment. *"Choosing rather to suffer affliction with the people of God, than to enjoy the pleasures of sin for a season."*—Hebrews 11:25

"My son, if sinners entice thee, consent thou not. My son, walk not thou in the way with them; refrain thy foot from their path."—Proverbs 1:10, 15 If you find yourself in a situation where you are being pressured to do something that you know is not right, do not follow the crowd. God will bless you for your dedication to Him, and those around you will admire you for your courage. *". . . ye have sinned against the LORD: and be sure your sin will find you out."*—Numbers 32:23

In addition to standing up for what is right and what your parents would desire you to stand up for, never hesitate to tell your parents everything that happened during a visit with a friend. Whether it was inappropriate conversation, wrong activities, or bad attitudes, share it with your parents. They will be grateful to you if you tell them right away rather than waiting for days on end.

As you spend time with your friends, never be afraid to stand up for God and His Word. Do what is right, whether it pleases your friends or not. Pleasing God should be your ultimate goal in your friendships and the truth is that they will admire you the more for it. Even fools admire people who stand up for what they know is right in the midst of circumstances.

"Be courteous to all, but intimate with few, and let those few be well tried before you give them your confidence."

—George Washington

A Strong Friendship

"As iron sharpeneth iron; so a man sharpeneth the countenance of his friend."—Proverbs 27:17

The people outside of my own home who I would consider my "best friends" are those who share a close relationship with me because of our love for Christ. In these friendships, we are not exactly alike; in fact, we are different in many ways, but our longing to grow in Christ is what binds us in that special, unique way. These are my friends who always have something to say about how God has been working in their lives. Our comments end up in lively conversation, and we each walk away "sharpened," encouraged, edified, and refined.

Over the years, you will have acquaintances, close friends, and people you simply enjoy talking with. You will probably notice if you have not already, that the closest friends you will ever have are the ones who encourage you in your walk with the Lord. It is wonderful to have a godly friend who sharpens you in your walk with Christ Jesus! *"Heaviness in the heart of man maketh it stoop: but a good word maketh it glad."*—*Proverbs 12:25*

Just like building your sibling relationships on a firm foundation, it is important to build your friendships on the Rock—the Lord Jesus Christ. *"A man shall not be established by wickedness: but the root of the righteous shall not be moved."*—*Proverbs 12:3* Friendships built on the Lord share one common tie that binds the two together in a beautiful relationship.

The Lord has blessed me with several friends who love Him and encourage me in my walk with Jesus Christ. One of them is a pen pal from Florida whom I have never met! Another goes to my church, and I get to visit with her on a regular basis. A couple of my godly, encouraging friends used to go to church with me but have since moved to different states, and our visits are few but very treasured! ☺ In all these friendships, however, I am "sharpened" every time I walk away from reading the letter, getting off the phone, or ending the conversation. I remember one Sunday when a friend and I literally walked around the church for hours just talking! Our conversation was not about the weather and the newest pet—it was about how God was working in our lives. I was so encouraged that night, and I know it is a memory I will keep forever. We must edify one another in the Word. The most wonderful and long-lasting friendship you will ever have is the one built on Jesus Christ. *"For where two or three are gathered together in My name, there am I in the midst of them."*—*Matthew 18:20*

> *"What, then, is the true way of loving one's friends? It is to love them in God, to love God in them; to love what He has made them; and to bear for love of Him what He has not made."*
>
> —Felelon

Becoming a Good Friend

"Even so ye, forasmuch as ye are zealous of spiritual gifts, seek that ye may excel to the edifying of the church."—1 Corinthians 14:12

Every girl longs to have a good friend—one who cares for others and serves in times of need. She wants to find a friend who will be loving, cheerful, godly, and sets a good example of a virtuous daughter. She wants a friend who is *faithful*.

"Therefore all things whatsoever ye would that men should do to you, do ye even so to them: for this is the law and the prophets."—Matthew 7:12 Instead of focusing on what your friends can be to you, try focusing on what you can be to them. By putting yourself last and others first, you will bless others in ways you never imagined.

"Do not waste time bothering whether you 'love' your neighbor; act as if you did. As soon as we do this we find one of the greatest secrets. When you are behaving as if you loved someone you will presently come to love him."
—C.S. Lewis

How can I be a good friend? I believe this passage in Colossians sums the question up! It contains excellent advice on being a good friend.

"Put on therefore, as the elect of God, holy and beloved, bowels of mercies, kindness, humbleness of mind, meekness, longsuffering; forbearing one another, and forgiving one another, if any man have a quarrel against any: even as Christ forgave you, so also do ye. And above all these things put on charity, which is the bond of perfectness. And let the peace of God rule in your hearts, to the which also ye are called in one body; and be ye thankful. Let the word of Christ dwell in you richly in all wisdom; teaching and admonishing one another in psalms and hymns and spiritual songs, singing with grace in your hearts to the Lord. And whatsoever ye do in word or deed, do all in the name of the Lord Jesus, giving thanks to God and the Father by Him."
—Colossians 3:12–17

There are several pointers in the above passage—we ought to be merciful, kind, humble, meek, and longsuffering. We should be able to forgive our friends for what they do wrong, and learn to bear the struggles that come into our friendships. Above all those things, we are to *love* our friends. If we have a true love for our friends, the qualities will more easily fall into place, and we will likely do them with the right heart and attitude. Additionally, by loving your friends you will have a longing to encourage them in the Lord. *"Knowledge puffeth up, but charity edifieth."*—*1 Corinthians 8:1*

The other thing that this verse reminds us is how important it is to encourage one another in the Lord. When you are with your friends, share what you read in your Bible that morning, or how God is working in your life. Build them up in the Lord and His ways.

"Two are better than one; because they have a good reward for their labour. For if they fall, the one will lift up his fellow: but woe to him that is alone when he falleth; for he hath not another to help him up. Again, if two lie together, then they have heat: but how can one be warm alone? And if one prevail against him, two shall withstand him; and a threefold cord is not quickly broken."—*Ecclesiastes 4:9–12*

Think of the strength you have in a friendship where both friends love the Lord and strive with all their might to serve Him! When Christ is the foundation and the main tie that bonds them, it is a threefold strength, and cannot be easily broken. By building your friendships on the Lord and His Word, you are headed for a long and pleasant relationship that will edify you in your walk with Christ. *"Let us therefore follow after the things which make for peace, and things wherewith one may edify another."*—*Romans 14:19*

"Let no corrupt communication proceed out of your mouth, but that which is good to the use of edifying, that it may minister grace unto the hearers. And grieve not the holy Spirit of God, whereby ye are sealed unto the day of redemption. Let all bitterness, and wrath, and anger, and clamour, and evil speaking, be put away from you, with all malice. And be ye kind one to another, tenderhearted, forgiving one another, even as God for Christ's sake hath forgiven you."—*Ephesians 4:29–32*

Just as you are not choosing friends that could be a bad influence on you, do not be a bad influence on your friend. Do not encourage her in wrong or speak about things that would not please, honor, and glorify God. If you do, you are not a faithful friend to her.

> *"Who we are is reflected in the people we choose as friends."*
> —Dr. Grace Ketterman

As you form friendships and strive to become a godly, encouraging friend, do all you can to encourage your friends in the Lord. Speak often of God's Word, pray together, and reflect on the Lord's goodness. *"Neither give heed to fables and endless genealogies, which minister questions, rather than godly edifying which is in faith: so do."*—1 Timothy 1:4

Friendship Evaluation 2:
What I am to My Friends—

- ♥ Do I encourage my friends to do what is right?
  ○ Yes   ○ No
- ♥ Do I encourage my friends to honor and obey their parents?
  ○ Yes   ○ No
- ♥ Am I a godly example of a virtuous daughter to my friends?
  ○ Yes   ○ No
- ♥ Can my friends trust that what I say is true and God-honoring?
  ○ Yes   ○ No
- ♥ Do I forgive and continue to love my friends when they wrong me?   ○ Yes   ○ No
- ♥ Do I share with my friends how God is working in my life and encourage them to do the same?
  ○ Yes   ○ No
- ♥ Do I pray with my friends, and discuss Scriptural truths with them?   ○ Yes   ○ No
- ♥ Do I share positive things about others with my friends?
  ○ Yes   ○ No
- ♥ Do I build my friendships on Jesus Christ, or around each other?

For Those Who've Gone Before

"That the aged women . . . may teach the young women . . ."
—Titus 2:3–4

I definitely do not consider myself "aged," and I am guessing none of my readers do either! ☺ However, I am familiar with many girls who are several years younger than me, and I think we "older" girls have a rare opportunity to encourage and bless the girls who are right behind us.

Our family went to the Grand Canyon in Arizona earlier this year. We chose to hike up a steep mountain (no, it was not actually in the Grand Canyon! ☺), but we started out late. As time went on and we got further, we were *tired*. We were *thirsty*. We were *hungry*. Despite our lack of preparation (we had no food or water—our life story), we really wanted to make it to the top. The further we hiked, the more breaks we excused as necessary. Right when we were all ready to give up and turn around, a hiker on his way down crossed our trail. He told us how much further, what the terrain was like, and his idea of whether or not he thought we could make it (since it was getting dark).

Just hearing his description of the trail encouraged us and helped us to make an appropriate decision. It was helpful to hear from one who had gone before us.

In the same way (or a similar way), is our relationship to girls younger than us. We may never know the influence we have on younger girls. When I was about twelve or thirteen, I was very encouraged by a dear older sister in Christ. She set a godly example for me of what it meant to be a virtuous daughter. I appreciated the advantage of watching a young woman who was right ahead of me! *"Let no man despise thy youth, but be thou an example of the believers, in word, in conversation, in charity, in spirit, in faith, in purity."*—1 Timothy 4:12

A couple of years ago, I befriended a young girl who was struggling in some areas. I thank God and praise His name because I really believe that He was able to use me in some ways to encourage her. She just needed to see someone who had gone before. She was looking up to me (what a sobering thought). Someone shared this sweet poem with *Virtuous Daughters,* and the words are challenging:

Model by Example

> A careful woman I ought to be
> A little girl follows me.
> I do not dare go astray,
> For fear she'll go the self same way.
> Not once can I escape her eyes
> Whate'er she sees me do she tries.
> Like me, she sees she's going to be
> That little girl who follows me.
> I must remember as I go
> Through summer sun and winter snow,
> I'm molding for the years to be
> That little girl who follows me.
> —unknown

So, to you older girls, remember that younger ones look up to you and are following your example. They long to be like you. Shine for Jesus and encourage them. Those early teen years can be difficult ones, and you may be the most encouraging person to help them along since you were just there yourself. *"Blessed be God, even the Father of our Lord Jesus Christ, the Father of mercies, and the God of all comfort; Who comforteth us in all our tribulation, that we may be able to comfort them which are in any trouble, by the comfort wherewith we ourselves are comforted of God. For as the sufferings of Christ abound in us, so our consolation also aboundeth by Christ."—2 Corinthians 1:3–5* Of course, being friends with younger girls is more sacrifice on your part, but think of the blessing you may be to them and the eternal benefits! ♥

An Extra Thought . . .

Bless Your Pen Pal!

From *Virtuous Daughters*, By Sarah Hulin

Whether it's Happy Birthday, Merry Christmas, or Just Because, these inexpensive mailable items are sure to brighten your pen pal's day.

- *Scripture cards*—Tuck business size cards in with your letters. What an enouragement!
- *Recipe cards*—with favorite recipes handwritten with love.
- *Bookmarks*—You can creatively construct bookmarks in many colors, ways, shapes, and forms. Bookmarks also make for good beginning cross stitch projects.
- *Pictures*—Your summer vacation, new pet, or recent photo of yourself all make for special letters.
- *Poems or Insights*—are always fun to share!
- *Flower seeds*—Sometimes I send Bluebonnet seeds to my out-of-state friends!
- *Stickers*—seem to enhance any letter or card.
- *Phone cards*—If you want to send a special birthday gift (especially to grandparents), prepaid pone cards are kind of neat.
- *Challenge!*—Why not challenge your pen pal by asking them to read a suggested book of the Bible with you? Hold each other accountable.
- *Gum*—You can mail a stick of chewing gum to a friend.
- How about sending a *package of Kool Aid or Tea* to your pal for a refreshing summer treat?

- *Confetti*—Cutting up paper into tiny squares and putting them in the bottom of your envelopes can be an exciting, fun way to surprise your friends when they open their letter.
- *Tape*—Record and send an audio tape. Sing happy birthday for birthdays or just record our letter instead of writing it.

Application...

"But be ye doers of the word, and not hearers only, deceiving your own selves."—James 1:22

Are your friends a godly or negative influence on your life? _____

Are you a part of any friendships that would not please God? If so, what should you do about them? _____
_____

Do you edify your friends in the Lord? If not, how can you begin to do that? _____
_____

List two Scriptures about friendships: _____
_____

Choose one of the following Scriptures to memorize and recite:

Ecclesiastes 4:9–12   *Matthew 18:20*
Ephesians 4:29–32   *Proverbs 22:24–25*
Colossians 3:12–17   *Proverbs 13:20*

Recited to: _____ Date: _____

Choose one of the following activities to work on:

- Write a note to one of your friends, and share with her what God has been teaching you lately, as well as asking her how God has been working in her life.
- Next time a friend displays a negative attitude about something godly (like siblings, parents' authority, etc.) encourage her in doing what is right.

–Chapter vii–
Becoming a Daughter of Honor

"A gracious woman retaineth honor: and strong men retain riches."
—*Proverbs 11:16*

Appreciating and Practicing
Values of Graciousness and Femininity

Consider the following responses to a woman who asked a simple question—

"Yeah, I'll be there at 12:00 or so, if I don't flop it and be late again." Sally stated as she put a piece of gum in her mouth and smacked away.

"Yes, ma'am, I should be there at 12:00. Thank you, Mrs. Smith." Dianna smiled as she gathered her things.

Which girl would you say is more gracious? _____

Desire for Honor

Every girl desires honor. She wants people to praise and admire her. How can she receive the honor and admiration she so longs for? In God's Word, we find that people honor a gracious woman. *"Strength and honor are her clothing; and she shall rejoice in time to come."*—Proverbs 31:25

In my first year of high school, I did a persuasive research paper. My goal in this paper was to persuade the reader that Dolley Madison set a good example for America's future First Ladies by being a gracious and generous First Lady. The books and articles I read about this woman quickly persuaded me that people indeed honored her for her gracious, loving heart.

If you desire honor, the key is not to try to draw attention by immodest dress or loud voice, but to be *gracious*, as God's Word says. Everyone honors a gracious woman, especially today, because there are so few. It is time to revive the neglected and forgotten graciousness and femininity in this world and in our young women! Gracious women are much more beautiful than independent, loud, prideful, and boisterous women are.

In fact, graciousness is not just an honor in a young woman; it is instruction from God's Word. *". . . teach the young women to be sober, to love their husbands, to love their children, to be discreet, chaste, keepers at home, good, obedient to their own husbands, that the word of God be not blasphemed."*—Titus 2:4–5

I will have to admit that I am not the perfect role model when it comes to being a gracious young lady (or anything else, for that matter!). Too often, I find myself acting in an ungraceful or unladylike manner. However, I am working on this area in my life, and as the Lord reveals things about it to me, I would like to pass some of that encouragement on to you.

What is Graciousness?

<u>Graciousness:</u> 1. Marked by kindness and courtesy 2. Graceful 3. Characterized by charm and good taste 4. Merciful
<u>Sober:</u> 3. Grave or serious 4. Marked by restraint: reasonable
<u>Grave:</u> 1. Very important 3. Solemn: dignified 4. Somber

The main reason, I believe, that many women and girls lack this quality—a gracious spirit—is because they are following feminists' ideas of trying to be equal with men by being physically strong. This so contradicts how the Scriptures describe women. She is to be gracious. Who is to be strong? The man. In a single verse (Proverbs 11:16) we are given two truths—woman is gracious; man is strong. *"A gracious woman retaineth honor: and strong men retain riches."—Proverbs 11:6*

All through God's Word, we see a similar cycle—the men were honored for their marvelous strength in battle and other activities. *"The glory of young men is their strength . . ."—Proverbs 20:29* The women were honored for their gracious and hospitable spirits, their beauty and dependency.

It was not long ago that people dishonored boisterous, independent women. Instead, young girls were raised and trained to be gracious keepers of the home. People appreciated their gracefulness and courtesy. Casual tones and flippant remarks were not allowed! They never raised their voices, and they looked presentable before going to town. They played quiet and graceful games as fun. They humbly served alongside their mothers, entertaining guests and doing work around the house. Never did a girl do something silly for attention. Instead, she was reserved and modest. These girls were thoughtful and loving. We live in a backwards culture—how different the world is today!

Contrary to today's masses of girls involved in highly competitive sports, young women in the 1700s and 1800s learned to sit still and do handwork. In many homes, there was an amount of time specifically set aside to be still and quiet. A profound truth that mothers taught their daughters was, "Least said, soonest mended."

The following is some advice one pioneer mother gave to her daughter:

> "*She wanted her girls* to know how to behave, to speak nicely in low voices and have gentle manners and always be ladies . . . [she] thought it best to keep themselves to themselves . . . She must be well-behaved and ladylike, and remember that a lady never did anything that could attract attention."
>
> —Laura Ingalls Wilder's *By the Shores of Silver Lake*

Back when girls grew up to be gracious and sober, it was the gossip of the town if a young girl was running and romping about. If a girl had what we now call the "tomboy" attitude, people considered the mother of this child to have not raised her daughter correctly. It was a shame to be ungracious!

What has happened? Why is all of this so different? Sad to say, the feminists' ideas have taken hold of many—even Christian—young women. They often do not realize it, because a "cute," independent girl is today's norm. However normal it is, this is not God's way. He is calling women to delight in being women! He is calling women to be grateful to Him for their design as women! Be gracious daughters, my sisters! There is such a need and call for it. Regardless of what the world is doing, God will honor you for your graciousness, and you may be surprised at outsiders who do too! Press on!

God's Beautiful Design

"I will praise Thee; for I am fearfully and wonderfully made: marvellous are Thy works; and that my soul knoweth right well."—Psalm 139:14

Satan has been victorious in getting some women to be unappreciative of the way God made them. They feel less important than men, thus believing that they can win more admiration and attention if they are more like the men. A woman's attitude and dress often indicate if she is gracious at heart or unhappy with the way God made her. The popular phrase, "girl power," is a perfect example of someone who feels she must be like the men to be important.

This is not true! Praise the Lord for the way He made you—for being a woman! In these days, it is easier said than done, but please do not fall into Satan's traps. Be grateful for your design, and encourage other girls to do the same. Right now, ponder on the words of this beautiful Psalm:

"O LORD, Thou hast searched me, and known me. Thou knowest my downsitting and mine uprising, Thou understandest my thought afar off. Thou compassest my path and my lying down, and art acquainted with all my ways. For there is not a word in my tongue, but, lo, O LORD, Thou knowest it altogether. Thou hast beset me behind and before, and laid Thine hand upon me. Such knowledge is too wonderful for me; it is high, I cannot attain unto it. Whither shall I go from Thy spirit? Or whither shall I flee from Thy presence? If I ascend up into heaven, Thou art there: if I make my bed in hell, behold, Thou art there. If I take the wings of the morning, and dwell in the uttermost parts of the sea; even there shall Thy hand lead me, and Thy right hand shall hold me. If I say, Surely the darkness shall cover me; even the night shall be light about me. Yea, the darkness hideth not from Thee; but the night shineth as the day: the darkness and the light are both alike to Thee. For Thou has possessed my reins: Thou hast covered me in my mother's womb. I will praise Thee; for I am fearfully and wonderfully made: marvellous are Thy works; and that my soul knoweth right well. My substance was not hid from Thee, when I was made in secret, and curiously wrought in the lowest parts of the earth. Thine eyes did see my substance, yet being unperfect; and in Thy book all my members were written, which in continuance were fashioned, when as yet there was none of them. How precious also are Thy thoughts unto me, O God! How great is the sum of them! If I should count them, they are more in number than the sand: when I awake, I am still with Thee. Surely Thou wilt slay the wicked, O God: depart from me therefore, ye bloody men. For they speak against Thee wickedly, and thine enemies take Thy name in vain. Do not I hate them, O LORD, that hate Thee? and am not I grieved with those that rise up against Thee? I hate them with perfect hatred: I count them mine enemies. Search me, O God, and know my heart: try me, and know my thoughts: and see if there be any wicked way in me, and lead me in the way everlasting." —Psalm 139

When a woman tries to be like a man in dress, attitude, activity, or strength, she is telling God that she is not happy with the way He made her, and she would rather be different. God did not make a mistake when He made you. Look back at *Genesis 1:27, 31*: "So God created man in His own image, in the image of God created He him; male and female created He them . . . And God saw everything that He had made, and, behold, it was very good . . ."

If you are struggling in word, thought, or deed with being content the way God made you, confess this sin to God, and ask His forgiveness. He will lovingly pick you up as the Good Shepherd and put you back where you belong. Forsake the ways of the worldly feminists. They are wrong and do not please God!

"I am most anxious to enlist everyone who can speak or write to join in checking this mad, wicked folly of 'Women's rights,' with all its attendant horrors, on which her poor feeble sex is bent, forgetting every sense of womanly feelings and propriety. Feminists ought to get a good whipping. Were woman to 'unsex' themselves by claiming equality with men, they would become the most hateful, heathen, disgusting of beings and would surely perish without male protection.

"I love peace and quiet, I hate politics and turmoil. We women are not made for governing, and if we are good women, we must dislike these masculine occupations." —Queen Victoria, 1870

The Weaker Vessel

"... giving honour unto the wife, as unto the weaker vessel."—1 Peter 3:7

Many girls have adopted the attitude that they must be strong like boys. The fact is that most women and girls are weaker in physical strength than men. They are also to perform different roles than men and boys. Remember the curse in Genesis:

Chapter Seven—Becoming a Daughter of Honor

> *"Unto the woman He said, I will greatly multiply thy sorrow and thy conception; in sorrow thou shalt bring forth children; and thy desire shall be to thy husband, and he shall rule over thee. And unto Adam He said, Because thou hast hearkened unto the voice of thy wife, and hast eaten of the tree, of which I commanded thee, saying, Thou shalt not eat of it: cursed is the ground for thy sake; in sorrow shalt thou eat of it all the days of thy life; thorns also and thistles shall it bring forth to thee; and thou shalt eat the herb of the field; in the sweat of thy face shalt thou eat bread, till thou return unto the ground; for out of it wast thou taken: for dust thou art, and unto dust shalt thou return. And Adam called his wife's name Eve; because she was the mother of all living."* —Genesis 3:16–20

Although it is less common these days, there was a time when men respected women and treated them as the "weaker vessel." It has been recorded that women traveling aboard the *Titanic* alone were titled "unprotected ladies," and placed under the responsibility of a man to keep them shielded from dangers. "Rebuke not an elder, but entreat him as a father; and the younger men as brethren; the elder women as mothers; the younger as sisters, with all purity. Honour widows that are widows indeed." —1 Timothy 5:1–2

While women and girls should be grateful for the honor they receive for being ladies, they should also not take it for granted. I have heard girls remind their brothers the "ladies first rule" when ice cream is being served. ☺ Or there is the girl who judges her brother for not offering her his seat. Remember that they are doing it as an honor to you, and you should be grateful for it, but not expectant.

So why should women receive so much honor? Men ought to receive honor also. God made women to be helpmeets for their husbands, and they should honor and serve them in a loving manner. Though she depends on him, she is quick to take care of him. She meets his needs.

As you strive to be a gracious girl, remember that you are the weaker vessel. Accept honor when it is due to you. Be careful to not be one who refuses seats and help carrying things when it is offered you. I know that this can be hard when inside you are just trying to be kind. There was a time when I had barely anything in my hand, and a young boy offered to carry it for me. He was trying to do me a favor, but I told him it was okay in a polite way. Then a look of disappointment came across his face—he was looking forward to doing something for someone, but I did not view it that way. I felt bad, and realized I was not being sensitive to the circumstances. God made men and boys to long to help the weaker vessels—women, girls, the elderly, and children—and we need to realize this! When we refuse their assistance (even in a kind way), it makes them feel of less value. It usually does not hurt to say, "Sure, thank you!" and hand something over. ☺

Also, remember to serve and honor your father and brothers. God expects you to do certain things for them, too. Treat them like men, just as they ought to treat you like a woman. *"And the LORD God said, It is not good that the man should be alone; I will make him an help meet for him."*—Genesis 2:18

Hidden Strength

"I can do all things through Christ which strengtheneth me."

—Philippians 4:13

Just because you are a gracious, dependent woman does not mean that you cannot do mighty things for God. In fact, you have strength to do wonderful things for His glory! I have read numerous biographies of missionary women who were in the midst of dangerous and trying circumstances, fleeing persecution, or facing it with courage. Where did their strength come from, especially since graciousness and femininity were evident in their life?

Although I will not tell her story, I will recommend reading about a missionary woman, Mary Slessor, because her life is an excellent example of a gracious and feminine woman who did mighty things for the Lord. Often her tasks were those of a man. Through Mary's life, I learned that a gracious woman can be strong. Yet it is only through the Lord. Miss Slessor understood this, and did not have the attitude of a feminist, but that of a woman who was willing to take any task the Lord set before her. In the following response of Mary Slessor, we see a woman who was strong in the Lord, humble, and gracious at heart:

A message was sent to Mary Slessor. It read, *"If this is a war, a woman is not likely to stop it."*

This godly woman's reply indicated strength and trust in the Lord, not in herself. *"You think only of the woman. You have forgotten the woman's God."*

Mary's answer to this question was an humble one, and a gracious one at that. She did not think of her own strength, for she knew that in her own strength she was very weak. She also knew, however, that Christ could work through her to do whatever task needed to be done to further His kingdom.

Gladys Aylward was another single missionary woman who demonstrated a feminine attitude and inward strength. After having been in China preaching about the living God for many years, she was surprisingly requested to stop a riot in the prison! Listening to the commotion for a moment did not ease Miss Aylward's hesitancy. She said, "That's a job for a man . . . Me? Why me? I am only a missionary woman. What could I do? Send for the soldiers."

The governor replied that the soldiers were frightened. After a brief debate, he earnestly persisted,

"How could they kill you? You say you have the living God inside of you . . . You have gone throughout our towns and villages preaching about the living God. You say He is with you always. If your words are true, then you can stop this riot." —These Are My People

That settled it for Gladys. She knew she had no choice but to trust in the Lord at this time, because if she did not practice what she had been preaching, the listeners would close their ears to the Gospel. As she approached the bloody courtyard, she prayed and sang hymns. God gave her amazing strength in which she was able to stop the riot and put all the men back in order. After this event, people were more open to her words than ever, because they wanted what she had—inward strength that comes *only* from the living God!

We must realize, like Mary Slessor and Gladys Aylward learned, that in ourselves we are weak. He always gives us strength in times of need. Nothing is possible without God, but everything is possible with Him! Praise the Lord and give Him the glory and honor!

Tomboy

"Here is a startling revelation: Men and women are different! . . . Let us speak the truth in love: It is wonderful to be a woman. It is glorious to be feminine." —Elizabeth Beall Phillips, *Verses of Virtue*

Ever since I can remember, I have disliked the term "tomboy" for girls. It just did not make sense. Why should a girl be proud of being like a boy? Though I will only touch on this, I wanted to remind my dear sisters to never glory in being or acting like a boy.

You may enjoy some activities that are normally "guy things," but do you realize that for a girl to do manly sports or recreation is common today? Why is it totally normal for girls to be involved in sports or hunting, fishing, etc., yet how often do you see men sewing, cooking, cross-stitching, decorating, etc.? Something is backwards, and many Christians fail to see Satan's subtle attempts to lead them astray.

As you grow and walk in the Lord, be grateful for the way God made you. If you find yourself fishing with your brother, or camping as a family, that is wonderful! I am not saying you can never play a game of volleyball or go hunting. Nevertheless, keep the gracious spirit and feminine attitude. I will also caution you to pray and seek your parents' counsel before regularly participating in rough, competitive sports. I realize that there are countless girls involved in sports today, but it has become an idol in our nation, and can be a stumbling block for young ladies in particular.

"Take some time and think about your thoughts, and if there is some discontentment, or some thoughts appear to be wrong, confess them and forsake them. God was very pleased to create us female, and we should delight in being women and doing womanly things."

—Suzan Zakula, *The Joy of Womanhood*

Aggressive and competitive sports are something that boasts of strength, not graciousness or femininity. I am not saying you can never be involved in a game; I am simply saying to be careful, and to be certain you do not adopt the boy's attitude. Remember to, as with everything, use discernment.

See what girls were encouraged to do in the 1800s:

> *"But you must be careful* to do nothing inconsistent with propriety—nothing out of character for you sex. . . . It would be unbecoming in you to play with the boys, or associate with them, any further than to engage in modest and sensible conversation . . . But the sports in which boys usually engage are improper for your sex . . . Choose for your recreations, those sports which are gentle and suited to your sex, not rough and roisterous."
>
> —Harvey Newcomb, *How To Be A Lady*

A Gracious Woman

Now then, we all know that it glorifies Christ when we show that we are grateful to Him for the way He designed us—girls! Specifically how can we honor Christ in this area? A true woman at heart who loves to be a woman is gracious—graceful—in everything she does. She proves this by the way that she speaks, eats, dresses, serves, and her overall manners. Even a woman's posture and rate of motion is an indicator of her heart's attitude.

I will admit that I am working on this part of my life, and seeking the Lord to guide and give me wisdom. Still, I know that people honor a gracious woman. There is a young lady in particular at our church who is a beautiful example of a gracious woman. Her outward appearance, her speech, everything that she does suggests that she is happy with the way God made her, and others honor her for her gracefulness.

Speech

"Let your speech be always with grace, seasoned with salt, that ye may know how ye ought to answer every man." —Colossians 4:6

Each of us have many opportunities to be gracious and shine for Jesus by the way we speak. To speak graciously is a combination of many things—tone of voice, word usage, and even facial expressions! These reflect if our speech is graceful and our attitude is godly.

Gracious speech is a soft, formal tone. It is not casual or silly. Instead of using slang words, it uses proper English. Try re-writing the following *ungracious* sentence with a more *gracious* approach:

"Yea, Lisa, get me a soda at the store. It's a really cool price— only a buck and a quarter for the biggest size they got!" ☺

Also, addressing the adults in your life can be done either in a respectful, formal manner, or in a casual, disrespectful manner. For a married woman named Lisa Smith, we would address her as "Mrs. Smith," rather than "Miss Lisa" or "Lisa."

Another aspect of gracious speech is the topic of speaking when necessary. There are times when it is not appropriate to speak about a certain subject and times when it is not appropriate to speak at all. Our gracious First Lady Dolley Madison was very skilled in starting lively conversations and being cautious at what became of them. It was said that she always carried a book with her when entering the drawing room for further fellowship. Her reason was quite simple,

"To have something not ungraceful to say, and if need be, to supply a word of talk." —First Lady Dolley Madison

She was also known for never speaking of the political issues of the day. She did not desire to participate in familiar gossip. She would frequently tell others,

"It is one of my sources of happiness, never to desire a knowledge of other people's business."

—First Lady Dolley Madison

Strive to use gracious phone and table manners. Often what is convenient is not necessarily good. It is easy to yell across the house for your dad when the phone is for him, but it is thoughtful to quickly and quietly give him the phone. It is easy to devour your meal before your mother even sits down, but it is much more considerate to wait for her to take a bite before you touch your own.

Try to learn what topics are appropriate and inappropriate to discuss with others. In some of the earlier years of our nation, it was considered rude and inconsiderate for men to discuss politics in the presence of women. In modern times, however, this standard has been sadly lowered to the point of anything can be discussed any time, anywhere, to anybody. Do not be deceived, dear girls, this is not for you! Show respect and good judgment in your speech habits.

Appearance

I remember seeing a woman in the store with her hair slicked back like a man's, and she was also wearing men's clothes. It was sad! A gracious woman or girl is sure to adorn her outward in a gracious manner that is not manly, but feminine. She wears clothes that are pressed and presentable. Most importantly, she seeks to draw people to her countenance and wears modest apparel. (See 1 Timothy 2:9–11.)

A woman's appearance includes her posture and "rate of motion." Stand up straight and tall! Slouching is unhealthy and not presentable. It will also make you feel more tired and less motivated.

Stay calm. There are only a few exceptions to running or shoving your way through a crowd—like when your two-year-old sister is running away. ☺ Even little things like getting in and out of a car matter. In "The Godly Daughter Checklist," by Renee Ellison, I read this practical but gracious approach to the process:

"[Getting] into and out of a car gracefully—by sitting sideways and then drawing my legs in afterwards." (I cannot say I do this every time I get in a vehicle, but it is a wonderful tip! ☺)

Another social manner would be the following that I never thought about until reading it from "The Godly Daughter Checklist":

> "*[I] am trying* not to chew gum because it looks like a cow chewing her cud and because it doesn't further a look of elegance in me."

I thought the tip on gum was humorous, but do you see the point? Be a daughter of gracefulness in all that you do because it brings honor to the Lord Jesus Christ. True beauty will come from your meek and gentle spirit, and God will bless you for it. *"Whose adorning let it not be that outward adorning . . . But let it be the hidden man of the heart . . . even the ornament of a meek and quiet spirit, which is in the sight of God of great price."*—1 Peter 3:3–4

Suggested Resources . . .

Books:
The Girl's Own Book, by Maria L. Child
The American Girl's Handy Book, by Lina & Adelia Beard (Both of these were written in the 1800s—they contain lots of gracious tips and games.)
The Little Woman, by Gladys Aylward
Daughters of Destiny, compiled and edited by Noelle Wheeler Goforth
The Birkenhead Drill, by Douglas Phillips
These are my People, by Mildred Howard
How To Be A Lady, by Harvey Newcomb

Activity:
  The "Game of Graces" or "La Grace" is a game we learned at a pioneer festival. The purpose of it was to teach girls graceful motion. I made one out of an embroidery hoop and four dowel-rods, but even sticks will work.
  Directions: Tie lace and ribbon to an embroidery hoop—fill it with feminine decorations! ☺ Using four sturdy sticks, the game is ready. Two girls stand a distance from each other, and, using the sticks in a scissor shape, they toss the hoop back and forth. Try to catch it . . . but be graceful! No leaping or flying through the air! ☺

An Extra Thought . . .
Maxims for Health & Gracefulness
Taken from: *The Girl's Own Book,* by Mrs. L. Maria Child

  EARLY rising, and the habit of washing frequently in pure cold water, are fine things for the health and complexion.
  WALKING and other out-of-door exercises, cannot be too much recommended to young people. Even skating, driving hoop, and other boyish sports may be practiced to great advantage by little girls, provided they can be pursued within the enclosure of a garden, or court; in the street, they would, of course, be highly improper. It is true, such games are rather violent, and sometimes noisy; but they tend to form a vigorous constitution; and girls who are habitually lady-like,

will never allow themselves to be rude and vulgar, even in play.

CHILDREN should eat simple food, and just as much of it as they need, and no more. Even the silly parrot will not eat merely to gratify her plate, when her appetite is satisfied. Many a pimpled face and aching head is produced by eating too much.

A TENDENCY to stoop should be early corrected. It is very destructive to health. This habit, together with the very ungraceful one of running the chin out, may be cured by the practice of walking the room frequently with a heavy folio volume balanced on the head, without the aid of the hands. The Egyptian women, who go down to the Nile to bring up heavy burdens of water on their heads, are remarkable for erect forms and majestic motions.

LITTLE girls should be careful, whether walking or sitting, to turn their feet out. The habit of turning the feet toward each other is extremely awkward. The practice of shrugging the shoulders is still more so: they should always be carried as low as possible.

Application...

"But be ye doers of the word, and not hearers only, deceiving your own selves."—James 1:22

Would others consider you a gracious girl who is content the way God made her? Why or why not?_____

Do you think the activities you enjoy please God?_____

What activities do you think of as being "masculine" and which do you think of as being "feminine"? _____

Which should you be and are you a part of?_____

List two Scriptures that encourage women in being *women*:
_____

Choose one of the following Scriptures to memorize and recite:

Genesis 2:18	*Proverbs 11:16*
Genesis 3:16–20	*Psalm 139:14*

Recited to: _____ Date: _____

Choose one of the following activities to work on:

- Wear dresses or skirts (feminine, modest apparel) for one week.

- Evaluate your activities. Are they God-honoring? Do they express gratitude for the way He created you?

–Chapter VIII–
Becoming a Daughter of Wisdom

"She openeth her mouth with wisdom; and in her tongue is the law of kindness." —Proverbs 31:26

Using My Tongue
To the Glory of the Father

"You are being so mean to me!" Esther scarcely noticed her sharp tongue as she walked away.

She left Hannah in tears. "I guess she's right, but she could have told me in a kinder way."

Esther did not hold her tongue, and the result was hurt feelings. How can she learn to control her words?

The Tongue's Power

"Death and life are in the power of the tongue: and they that love it shall eat the fruit thereof."—Proverbs 18:21

The tongue is a weapon or medicine that you carry with you twenty-four hours a day, seven days a week. It can speak gracious words of wisdom and love, or it can put out offensive words of hatred and folly. It can either encourage and strengthen someone, or it can hurt and dishearten a person. James gives us a vivid description of this powerful weapon:

"For in many things we offend all. If any man offend not in word, the same is a perfect man, and able also to bridle the whole body. Behold, we put bits in the horses' mouths, that they may obey us; and we turn about their whole body. Behold also the ships, which though they be great, and are driven of fierce winds, yet are they turned about with a very small helm, whithersoever the governor listeth. Even so the tongue is a little member, and boasteth great things. Behold, how great a matter a little fire kindleth! And the tongue is a fire, a world of iniquity: so is the tongue among our members, that it defileth the whole body, and setteth on fire the course of nature; and it is set on fire of hell. For every kind of beasts, and of birds, and of serpents, and of things in the sea, is tamed, and hath been tamed of mankind: But the tongue can no man tame; it is an unruly evil, full of deadly poison. Therewith bless we God, even the Father; and therewith curse we men, which are made after the similitude of God. Out of the same mouth proceedeth blessing and cursing. My brethren, these things ought not so to be. Doth a fountain send forth at the same place sweet water and bitter? Can the fig tree, my brethren, bear olive berries? either a vine, figs? so can no fountain both yield salt water and fresh." —James 3:2–12

The tongue is powerful, indeed. In ourselves, it is impossible to control. Through Jesus Christ, however, we can take it under control and speak words of wisdom that honor and glorify the Lord. Let us examine Scriptures that help us to see the power of the tongue.

The Bible describes the virtuous woman as someone who speaks wisdom and kindness. *"She openeth her mouth with wisdom; and in her tongue is the law of kindness."*—Proverbs 31:26 This woman knows how to use her tongue wisely and to the glory of God. She knows when to speak, and when to refrain from speaking. *"If any man among you seem to be religious, and bridleth not his tongue, but deceiveth his own heart, this man's religion is in vain."*—James 1:26

Harm or Health?

"There is that speaketh like the piercings of a sword: but the tongue of the wise is health."—Proverbs 12:18

We can never take back the words we speak. Sometimes they are healthy words that encourage and refresh others. Less desirable are the times they are words that hurt and discourage a person. I remember a time when I made a joke that I thought was funny, but I hurt the person I was talking about. I can never take back those words, but I want to work harder at speaking kind, pleasant, and *healthy* words!

What about you? Here is a little scenario:

> Your friend Alyssa struggles with slothfulness. You know that because when you call at 9:00 in the morning, she is still in bed. She has also told you how she struggles in this area, and she wants to do better. Honestly, you simply do not know how to help her.
>
> One day when you and Alyssa are together, you comment that you were sewing a dress at 7:00 in the morning. She says a little shamefully, "Oh, I was still asleep at that time!"
>
> You say rudely, "Well, you're just a sluggard, Alyssa, and you need to start getting up earlier like a virtuous woman does!"
>
> OR you could say, "Well, you know what helps me to get up: I set my alarm clock for 6:00, and as soon as I hear it I jump out of bed

without hesitation so I will not lay down and fall back asleep. Rising early can be a hard habit to form, but it sure is worth it!" ☺

Sometimes we are engaged in conversation, and the opportunity arises for us to use our tongue as an encouragement. Someone may express worry, fear, or anxiety about something. Be ready to encourage them in the Lord and in His Word! *"Heaviness in the heart of man maketh it stoop: but a good word maketh it glad."*—Proverbs 12:25

The best way to encourage someone is to share God's promises with him. *"For the word of God is quick, and powerful, and sharper than any twoedged sword, piercing even to the dividing asunder of soul and spirit, and of the joints and marrow, and is a discerner of the thoughts and intents of the heart."*—Hebrews 4:12 A few years ago, I received a phone call from a girl I barely knew; she was crying and shared that her cat had just been killed by some dogs. I was speechless. What did she want me to say? I told her I was so sorry, and I hoped that she would feel better soon. Now I realize the most encouraging thing I told her was that I would be praying for her. I wish I had prayed *with* her—this is some of the best encouragement. When a friend is going through a trial, tell her you will pray for her, and do it.

There have been times when a friend shared shocking news with me, and I did not know the right words to say. One good thing to do is simply listen. If she is seeking counsel or encouragement, give it to her in a loving way. Share with her the promises of God—the only certainty she really has in life. Bless her with words of wisdom, truth, and love. *"Every word of God is pure: He is a shield unto them that put their trust in Him."*—Proverbs 30:5

Kind and Pleasant Words

"Pleasant words are as an honeycomb, sweet to the soul, and health to the bones."—Proverbs 16:24

Speak words of kindness to people on a daily basis. I always appreciate meeting pleasant people in town who make cheery comments like, "Hello, how are you today?" Cheerful hearts and attitudes are the best. *"A merry heart maketh a cheerful countenance: but by sorrow of the heart the* spirit is broken."—*Proverbs 15:13*

Recently we were at the store getting copies of *Virtuous Daughters*. It had been a stressful day of running errands, and now we were having problems with the printing. While waiting, however, I was encouraged by an elderly woman who entered the store. She did not try to fix our problems—she was unaware that we even had any! But she wore a friendly smile and spoke kind, pleasant words. I doubt she will ever know she encouraged me to be happy that day.

You may never know, either, how much you can help make a heart merry again! This may be by simply standing in line at the local grocery store with a cheerful smile and happy attitude. Your love for Jesus Christ and His shining through you can really excite someone about life! The few words you speak to the lady working the cash register could make her day! You never know how the Lord will work through you as you speak kind and pleasant words.

When you leave someone's home after a visit, thank them for their hospitality. Show appreciation to your authorities, and give words of love to your parents and family. Kind and pleasant words are not nearly as plenteous as they ought to be, but let us purpose to create more of them and brighten more people's days! *"A man hath joy by the answer of his mouth: and a word spoken in due season, how good is it!"* —*Proverbs 15:23*

The Lip of Truth

"Keep thy tongue from evil, and thy lips from speaking guile. Depart from evil, and do good; seek peace, and pursue it."—*Psalm 34:13–14*

To speak a lie is a serious sin, as we see all throughout God's Word. There are countless warnings against this act in the Bible, as can be evident by the two verses that repeat the same truth in a single chapter: *"A false witness shall not be unpunished, and he that speaketh lies shall not escape . . . A false witness shall not be unpunished, and he that speaketh lies shall perish."*—*Proverbs 19:5,9* To lie may seem convenient for a time, but it simply tangles you into a bigger mess. *"The getting of treasures by a lying tongue is a vanity tossed to and fro of them that seek death."*—*Proverbs 21:6*

The good news is, however, that: *"The lip of truth shall be established for ever: but a lying tongue is but for a moment."*—Proverbs 12:19 Do you wisely speak the truth? If so, the Lord will reward you for that. If people know you for a lying tongue, however, your pleasure is temporary, and you will fall.

God delights in truth because He is truth and can speak no lie. Do you want your Heavenly Father to delight in you? Speak words of truth that cannot be denied. *"Lying lips are abomination to the LORD: but they that deal truly are His delight."*—Proverbs 12:22

To speak lies is something that God hates (see Proverbs 6:16–17), and it is very ungracious. Be ashamed to speak a lie or try to deceive someone. You are always better off to tell the truth. Telling a lie may seem to get you out of trouble for the moment, but never forget that *"your sin will find you out."* (See Numbers 32:23.)

A False Witness

"A false witness shall not be unpunished, and he that speaketh lies shall not escape . . . A false witness shall not be unpunished, and he that speaketh lies shall perish." —Proverbs 19:5,9

To "bear a false witness" is to tell a lie about someone. God despises this sin so much that He included it as one of the Ten Commandments. *"Thou shalt not bear false witness against thy neighbour."*—Exodus 20:16 *"Neither shalt thou bear false witness against thy neighbor."*—Deuteronomy 5:20

Every girl who reads this should know better than to speak lies and make up untrue stories about someone simply to get them in trouble. It is not only wrong, but it stirs up malice and hatred. In the following passage, we see how much God is displeased when one of His children becomes a false witness.

"These six things doth the LORD hate: yea, seven are an abomination unto Him: a proud look, a lying tongue, and hands that shed innocent blood, an heart that deviseth wicked imaginations, feet that be swift in running to mischief, a false witness that speaketh lies, and he that soweth discord among brethren." —Proverbs 6:16–19

Always beware to never fall into the trap of spreading untrue gossip about others. Just because you are on bad terms with someone does not give you the right to spread disgraceful lies about him. Instead, make the wrong into right.

Gossip

A false witness can be associated with a gossiper. Gossip is information, true or untrue, that someone spreads about others behind their back. A girl who gossips is one who will tell you all about the Jones family and how they recently did something bad, or about the latest problems in church. She often takes a fact and twists it around so that it comes out in a negative manner.

The Bible gives us plain warning against such a sin. *"He that goeth about as a talebearer revealeth secrets: therefore meddle not with him that flattereth with his lips."—Proverbs 20:19* You may be tempted to hang around a girl who is giving out interesting information about someone else, but refrain from giving in! If you do overhear something about someone else, do not tell other people unless it is necessary and accurate information.

"Speak not evil one of another, brethren. He that speaketh evil of his brother, and judgeth his brother, speaketh evil of the law, and judgeth the law: but if thou judge the law, thou art not a doer of the law, but a judge."—James 4:11

There are times when one person starts speaking badly of another. This is not edifying each other! If you are talking to your friend Lisa and she tells you, "I can't believe that Grace told that outright lie to Mr. and Mrs. Smith! Can you believe it? She is so sinful!"

Lisa may be sure that Grace did this, and you may know the same information, but you could respond in this manner: "That is sad. We could pray for her. But Grace does have godly character qualities we can look up to. Have you ever noticed how diligent she is in her work?"

You *do* need to accept the fact that someone is doing something wrong. But do not judge them. Instead, pray for them and find the positive qualities in them. As my pastor puts it, "Hate the sin; love the sinner."

"For our exhortation was not of deceit, nor of uncleanness, nor in guile: but as we were allowed of God to be put in trust with the gospel, even so we speak; not as pleasing men, but God, which trieth our hearts. For neither at any time used we flattering words, as ye know, nor a cloak of covetousness; God is witness."

—1 Thessalonians 2:3–5

Flattery

To flatter someone is to praise them too much. It can hurt the person you are praising, because it may tempt them to become prideful in their accomplishments. Girls can be guilty of this flaw:

> *Grace was showing Leslie the doily she had embroidered for her sister for Christmas. Leslie holds it and boisterously says, "Oh it is so beautiful! You did an excellent job! How did you do it? Oh I wish I could do something this wonderful! You are so talented in crocheting! If my mother could only see this!" She continues to flatter Grace's work until Grace either feels that her words of praise and admiration are hollow and insincere or is deceived into thinking prideful thoughts about herself.*

The truth is that flattery is often insincere. *"But let your communication be, Yea, yea; Nay, nay: for whatsoever is more than these cometh of evil." —Matthew 5:37* While I am not saying it is wrong to praise someone in their hard work (I think that is important—we should encourage our friends in good, useful skills), too much can be *too much*. Making a big show of something and drawing attention is an example of too much. A few short sentences and an admiring smile is enough to encourage Grace in her work. *"For neither at any time used we flattering words, as ye know, nor a cloak of covetousness; God is witness."—1 Thessalonians 2:5*

> *Speaking much is a sign of vanity.*
> *—Raleigh*

I appreciate Mary Landis's explanation in her book, *Dear Princess*:

"Exaggerated exclamations could only be

called insincere flattery. This is too common among young girls where the desire to please and be well-liked leads them to gushiness and exaggeration in their compliments to others."

Using Words Sparingly

"He that hath knowledge spareth his words: and a man of understanding is of an excellent spirit. Even a fool, when he holdeth his peace, is counted wise: and he that shutteth his lips is esteemed a man of understanding."
—*Proverbs 17:27–28*

This is one of the most profound yet unheeded truths we find in God's Word! The Lord honors a girl or woman who is wise in knowing when to speak and when to be silent. Jesus Christ is our ultimate example. When He was being sentenced to die, our Lord used few but truthful and necessary words. Questions were pouring from all directions, yet He knew to hold His tongue at the right time.

"And Jesus stood before the governor: and the governor asked Him, saying, Art Thou the King of the Jews? And Jesus said unto him, Thou sayest. And when He was accused of the chief priests and elders, He answered nothing."
—*Matthew 27:11–12*

In the first three Gospels, we find this same account: The governor questioned Jesus, and He answered in few words. They accused Him, and He wisely chose to remain silent. This would have been a convenient time for Christ to defend Himself; after all, He did and does have power over everything. (See John 19:11.) Yet He was obedient to His Father in Heaven, and He wisely chose to remain silent. *"In the multitude of words there wanteth not sin: but he that refraineth his lips is wise. The tongue of the just is as choice silver: the heart of the wicked is little worth."*—*Proverbs 10:19–20*

Are you wise in choosing your words? There are times when the best thing to do is remain silent. There are also times to use our words sparingly—just a few is plenty. ☺ *"A word fitly spoken is like apples of gold in pictures of silver."*—*Proverbs 25:11* Too often, I have opened my mouth and hurt someone's feel-

> "Learn to hold thy tongue; five words cost Zacharias forty weeks of silence."
> —Fuller

ings, embarrassed myself, said something that I thought was true but later realized was not, the list goes on! When we speak hastily, the results are often unpleasant. We are unconscious of what we say when we talk too fast.

Many times when we have left a fellowship or party, or I have just set down the telephone from talking, I always feel better when I have said fewer words! ☺ When I rattled on about something, however, I go away thinking, "I said too much. That sounded weird. This probably wasn't even true, etc." Proverbs 13:3 comes to mind: *"He that keepeth his mouth keepeth his life: but he that openeth wide his lips shall have destruction."*

As you go from day to day, remember that to say too little is often better than to say too much. The Scriptures support this idea many times, and Jesus Himself practiced the principle of using words wisely and sparingly. *"But I say unto you, That every idle word that men shall speak, they shall give account thereof in the day of judgment. For by thy words thou shalt be justified, and by thy words thou shalt be condemned."—Matthew 12:36*

"To everything there is a season, and a time to every purpose under the heaven . . . a time to keep silence, and a time to speak."—Ecclesiastes 3:1, 7 Speak each word wisely and to the glory of the Father!

Gracious Speech

Lastly, we find that God desires us to speak graciously. A girl should speak in a gracious tone and use wholesome, edifying words. She smiles as she communicates to someone and she speaks softly, not trying to draw attention or put on a big show. People honor her for this. *"He that loveth pureness of heart, for the grace of his lips the king shall be his friend."—Proverbs 22:11*

A daughter who is speaking graciously does not use slang or casual words. Instead, she is more formal and appropriate. Common terms such as "cool" and "dude" are not a part of her graceful vocabulary. She replaces them with wholesome words that are grammatically correct and honoring. *"A wholesome tongue is a tree of life: but perverseness therein is a breach in the spirit."—Proverbs 15:4*

Never forget that *"Death and life are in the power of the tongue: and they that love it shall eat the fruit thereof."—Proverbs 18:21*

–Psalm 12–

"HELP, LORD; for the godly man ceaseth; for the faithful fail from among the children of men. They speak vanity every one with his neighbor: with flattering lips and with a double heart do they speak. The LORD shall cut off all flattering lips, and the tongue that speaketh proud things: who have said, With our tongue will we prevail; our lips are our own: who is lord over us? For the oppression of the poor, for the sighing of the needy, now will I arise, saith the LORD; I will set him in safety from him that puffeth at him. The words of the LORD are pure words: as silver tried in a furnace of earth, purified seven times. Thou shalt keep them, O LORD, Thou shalt preserve them from this generation for ever. The wicked walk on every side, when the vilest men are exalted."

Suggested Resources . . .

Books:
Least Said, Soonest Mended, by Agnes Giberne
Little Daisy and the Swearing Class, unknown

An Extra Thought . . .

The Dog Puppy

"He that hath knowledge spareth his words . . . Even a fool, when he holdeth his peace, is counted wise: and he that shutteth his lips is esteemed a man of understanding."—Proverbs 17:27a, 28 This verse ought to train us girls so much! We have been writing about speaking things that please the King, but did you know that there are times it pleases the King for us to not speak at all? Because many girls are "chatter boxes," it is an important concept for us to grasp.

As we see all throughout God's Word, particularly in the Proverbs, there are many times when it is wisest to remain silent. Although I am doing better, I used to struggle in this area. All too soon, I would open my mouth, and—out it came. Whether I spoke an unnecessary word or an unkind word, I later regretted not "holding my peace."

In addition to gossip (which is wrong as you know), we have unnecessary words: *"But I say unto you, That every idle word that men shall speak, they shall give account thereof in the day of judgment. For by thy words thou shalt be justified, and by thy words thou shalt be condemned."—Matthew 12:36–37*

Here is a little story in which we see one way this principle is often violated:

"The Dog Puppy"

"I am going to tell you a story of a dog puppy," Dad said one afternoon with his family around him. But before he could continue, Kathryn chimed in,

"Dad, there's no such thing as a 'dog puppy'—there are dogs and puppies though." Dad laughed a little as he adjusted his seat,

"That's true, Kathryn. Maybe we should say puppy, although it grew to be a dog. But anyway, Bryan was about seven years old when we decided to buy him a puppy. We thought . . ." But Dad couldn't continue without Kathryn's information,

"Actually, Dad," she looked at her younger brother, "Bryan was eight when we got Rover."

"Oh, okay," Dad sighed but continued. "We thought Bryan would really like to have a collie since he always loved the 'Lassie' movies . . ." Kathryn opened her mouth again,

"Dad, are you sure Lassie was a collie? I think he was a golden retriever."

"No, I think—actually, I know—that Lassie was a collie, because . . ."

"But, Dad, I'm sure that Lassie was a golden retriever because . . . "

The family sat looking at Dad and Kathryn, waiting for the rest of the story.

"Never mind that," Dad looked agitated. "Let me finish the story please. Okay, now where was I? Oh, yes, since Bryan loved Lassie, we decided he would probably love a collie. So we took the van to a . . . " Dad was interrupted again.

"No, Dad," Kathryn said, "we had a small car back then—I remember."

"Right, but, well, we took the car to the pet store and bought a beautiful collie. He was just a pup and the man sold him to us . . . " Again, Kathryn had to say something.

"Dad, I think it was a lady."

"Well, yes, the lady sold him to us for only $200!" Dad said with a grin.

"Well, with tax, I think we paid about $220 or so." Kathryn said. Dad gave up the story in hopeless despair.

Wow! What a story! It would have been anyway, but Kathryn ruined it for us. All the details that she corrected her father on really ruined what could have made for an excellent story! And instead of receiving the attention she had expected, we no doubt consider her a fool.

So, dear girls, be ever so careful to not use words when they are useless in this way, especially in the instances just described. They are full of pride and rooted in selfishness. Of course there will be times when someone is telling a story and you need to correct them, but little, unimportant details can be left alone. Only the things that are necessary should be dealt with. *"A wise son maketh a glad father: but a foolish son is the heaviness of his mother."—Proverbs 10:1*

Application...

"But be ye doers of the word, and not hearers only, deceiving your own selves."—James 1:22

Are you wise in discerning when to speak, and when to not? In what ways can you improve on this? _____
_____
_____

Is your speech gracious and kind rather than cocky and rude? Does it denote a feminine girl? _____
_____

List two Scriptures that talk about speech: _____
_____

Choose one of the following Scriptures to memorize and recite:

Psalm 12   *James 4:11*
Matthew 12:36–37 *James 3:2–13*
Proverbs 13:3   *Proverbs 18:21*

Recited to: _____ Date: _____

Choose one of the following activities to work on:

- Make a list of slang or worldly words that you should remove from your vocabulary and find wholesome, pleasant replacements for them.

- Strive to speak to others with a low, soft tone, and gracious attitude. Call adults by their proper names.

–Chapter ix–
Becoming a Daughter of Beauty

"For all things are for your sakes, that the abundant grace might through the thanksgiving of many redound to the glory of God. For which cause we faint not; but though our outward man perish, yet the inward man is renewed day by day." —2 Corinthians 4:15–16

**Appreciating Beauty of the Heart
And Adorning My Outward Appearance
To the Glory of the Father**

A young woman passed by with beautiful hair and the nicest set of clothes. Clara simply shook her head. "I wish I was a tenth of what she is in beauty . . . but I'm not! What can I do about it?"

Clara was coveting the outward appearance of someone else. It is natural for her to long to be beautiful, but she must retain a godly, righteous focus.

Beauty, Beauty!

Almost every woman has a natural longing to be beautiful. This is evident not only today but in some of the earliest generations, and the desire has continued throughout the ages. Long ago, women would adorn themselves with frilly dresses and rich jewels. They would spend time fixing their hair to be comely and would gaze at themselves in looking glasses to be satisfied.

Today women still spend money on the "coolest" clothes in style or on pounds of makeup (☺) and hair gadgets. They spend hours in the mirror adorning themselves to be attractive. Accordingly, they feel that their time and money is paid off when someone comments on their outward appearance.

This *desire* is natural and not sin in itself. Yet some women take the longing to be outwardly beautiful too far, and others are simply deceived. (Remember that *favor* is deceitful according to Proverbs 31:30) One of the differences between the women of today and yesterday, in their goal to be beautiful, is that most women of the past adorned themselves in ways that expressed gratitude for their femininity, and many of the women today are adorning themselves in ways that put their design to shame.

The other difference I might add is that long ago, most women did not spend half their life in front of the mirror. They knew what was too far. They were hard workers, and if they were sun burned, cut up, or there was a hair out of place, it was not the end of the world. Godly women strove to be presentable, but understood that *inward* is far more important than *outward*.

While your desire to be beautiful is good, keep it pure. The clothes and makeup, jewels, and hair gadgets are tempting, but some of them are not good. Many of the clothes that you find today are immodest, and there is a limit in buying even things like hair clips and makeup when it comes to time, money, and your "level" of "I must have it!"

Let us search out God's Word and see what He has to say about the outward appearance, and how we can adorn ourselves to the glory of the Father.

> *"I will greatly rejoice* in the LORD, my soul shall be joyful in my God; for He hath clothed me with the garments of salvation, He hath covered me with the robe of righteousness, as a bridegroom decketh himself with ornaments, and as a bride adorneth herself with her jewels. For as the earth bringeth forth her bud, and as the garden causeth the things that are sown in it to spring forth; so the LORD GOD will cause righteousness and praise to spring forth before all the nations."* —Isaiah 61:10–11

Fading Beauty

"For all flesh is as grass, and all the glory of man as the flower of grass. The grass whithereth, and the flower thereof falleth away."—1 Peter 1:24

The thing that many girls fail to realize in their teen years is that their outward beauty is fading and will continue in that manner. It is true that you may become more beautiful over the years for a while, but at some point, all your outward beauty will begin to degrade and you will either be content and undisturbed or agitated and covetous. The amount of time and thought you put into your outward now will determine what your attitude will be tomorrow. *". . . thou makest his beauty to consume away like a moth: surely every man is vanity. Selah."* —Psalm 39:11

"Woe to the crown of pride, to the drunkards of Ephraim, whose glorious beauty is a fading flower, which are on the head of the fat valleys of them that are overcome with wine!"—Isaiah 28:1 You have probably been described as a beautiful flower before, blooming by the day. But do you realize that one day that beauty will fade just as a flower fades and withers away?

I can recall a beautiful wedding shower, and the theme was the early to mid-1900s. The bride had pictures framed of her grandparents and relatives from that time. My mother and I gazed at the precious photographs as the bride's mother described each one to us. She pointed out of the crowd the bride's grandmother and showed us her picture on the wall. She had definitely been a beautiful woman, but looking at her decades later, she had aged and wrinkled. What had become even more beautiful over the years, however, was her heart. *"For He knoweth our frame; He remembereth that we are dust. As for man, his days are as grass: as a flower of the field, so he flourisheth. For the wind passeth over it, and it is gone; and the place thereof shall know it no more. But the mercy of the LORD is from everlasting to everlasting upon them that fear Him, and His righteousness unto children's children."*—Psalm 103:14–17

2 Corinthians 4:16 tells us that though our outward fades and perishes, our inward can become more and more beautiful each day. The fading of the outward is a given—nothing can stop it. However, the heart—the inward—has much potential to become more beautiful and lovely as the years pass. While the outward is temporal, the inward is eternal. To which part are you going to devote the most focus? *"And when the chief Shepherd shall appear, ye shall receive a crown of glory that fadeth not away."*—1 Peter 5:4

The following from *Daughters of Destiny* is quite insightful:

> *"No gift from heaven* is so general and so widely abused by woman as the gift of beauty. In many cases, it makes her thoughtless, giddy, vain, proud, frivolous, selfish, low, and mean. I think I have seen more girls spoiled by beauty than by any other one thing. 'She is beautiful, and she knows it,' is as much as to say she is spoiled. A beautiful girl is very likely to believe she was made to be looked at. And believe and acting thus, she soon becomes good for nothing else, and when she comes to be a middle-aged woman she is that weakest, most sickening of all human things—a faded beauty. Outward beauty is shallow—only skin deep; fleeting—only reigning for a season. But inward beauty will last forever.
>
> *"If you desire to be admired and beloved, be an example of beautiful

womanhood and cultivate the virtues of the heart. Wealth may surround you with its blandishments, and beauty, learning, or talents, may give you admirers, but love and kindness alone can captivate the heart. Whether you live in a cottage or a palace, these graces can surround you with perpetual sunshine, making you, and all those around you, happy.

"Seek then, fair daughters, the possession of that inward grace, whose essence shall fragrance and vitalize the affections, adorn the countenance, make sweet the voice, and impart a hallowed beauty throughout your very being."

By focusing on the inward, you are polishing and beautifying your *life* instead of just your body. You are making your heart valuable and your attitude lovely. When I meet a young lady who has *truly* made her life beautiful, I scarcely notice her outward appearance. Her cheerful smile and meek and gentle spirit are what draw me to her, and that is what I admire in her. God blesses women and girls who strive to beautify their hearts—daughters of the King. *"So shall the king greatly desire thy beauty: for He is thy Lord; and worship thou Him . . . The king's daughter is all glorious within: her clothing is of wrought gold."*—Psalm 45:11, 13

What God Sees

God is clear in His Word that He is more concerned about the *heart* of man than the *body* of man. When Samuel was choosing someone to be the next king of Israel, God gave this instruction:

"Look not on his countenance, or on the height of his stature; because I have refused him: for the LORD seeth not as man seeth; for man looketh on the outward appearance, but the LORD looketh on the heart." —1 Samuel 16:7

God does not devote His sole focus on the outward appearance. This does not mean that the outward appearance is irrelevant in life, but it does mean that you ought to be spending more time in God's Word than you are in front of the mirror adorning your outward. Why? In the end, when it has all been said and done, the amount of time you spent in God's Word and getting to know Him will mean everything. It will be all that matters. *"Favour is deceitful and beauty is vain: but a woman that feareth the LORD, she shall be praised. Give her of the fruit of her hands; and let her own works praise her in the gates."*—Proverbs 31:30–31

Isaiah speaks of our Lord Jesus Christ and says, *"For He shall grow up before him as a tender plant, and as a root out of dry ground: He hath no form nor comeliness; and when we shall see Him, there is no beauty that we should desire Him."*—Isaiah 53:2 People were not attracted by Jesus' clothes. They were drawn to His character—His meekness. What is it about you that draws people to you?

> *"Charm is deceitful.* Sometimes it is pretending something you are not. Beauty is vain—it fades. Our bodies are temples of the Holy Spirit. We should keep them clean and present ourselves in the best way we can. But if we spend more time dressing up the external than we do the internal (putting on Christ, the full armor of God, etc.), we are out of balance. Remember the best thing to put on our external is a smile . . . Dear virtuous daughters, don't be fooled by the world. Seek first His kingdom and His righteousness, and all these other things will be added unto you." —Mrs. Donna Ewing, in *Virtuous Daughters*

A friend once shared that her goal is to spend more time in the mirror of God's Word than she does in the physical mirror. While the outward is important and we should not neglect it, our sole focus should not be outward beauty. *"Judge not according to the appearance, but judge righteous judgment."*—John 7:24

First Cleansing

The outward and inward can be two similar or very different things. Our Lord must be grieved when a young woman spends much time to make her outward appearance beautiful but fails to work on her heart.

"And the Lord said unto him, Now do ye Pharisees make clean the outside of the cup and the platter; but your inward part is full of ravening and wickedness. Ye fools, did not he that made that which is without make that which is within also?"—Luke 11:39–40

God desires that we first work on the heart—the inward. Then we may adorn the outward to the glory of the Father. I have always felt that I should not be spending a lot of time on my outward appearance if my heart is not right.

"Woe unto you, scribes and Pharisees, hypocrites! For ye make clean the outside of the cup and of the platter, but within they are full of extortion and excess. Thou blind Pharisee, cleanse first that which is within the cup and platter, that the outside of them may be clean also. Woe unto you, scribes and Pharisees, hypocrites! For ye are like unto whited sepulchers, which indeed appear beautiful outward, but are within full of dead men's bones, and of all uncleanness. Even so ye also outwardly appear righteous unto men, but within ye are full of hypocrisy and iniquity."—Matthew 23:25–28

The Lord is particularly pleased with daughters who long to serve Him with all their hearts. He sees His faithful followers as being truly beautiful, regardless of what the world thinks of them. *". . . How beautiful are the feet of them that preach the gospel of peace, and bring glad tidings of good things!"*—Romans 10:15

Representatives of Christ

"Ye are our epistle written in our hearts, known and read of all men: forasmuch as ye are manifestly declared to be the epistle of Christ ministered by us, written not with ink, but with the Spirit of the living God; not in tables of stone, but in fleshy tables of the heart." —2 Corinthians 3:2–3

Representatives of our President do not fail to attend to their outward appearance. They represent the President and understand that they must press their clothes, as well as keep their bodies clean. This does not mean that they spend all their time on their appearance, for they do serve the President, but part of their service is attending to their outward so that the President is well represented.

You are a servant of the Lord Jesus Christ! You represent Him when you go to the store, when you attend church, when you entertain guests at your home, and even when you are simply sitting in the backyard for a rest. Your outward is an indicator of what is inside; it is a "frame for the message," as I have read.

This does not mean that you have to wear a starched, elaborate dress when cleaning up the yard. You are to use discernment in finding the appropriate clothing for the appropriate time. Going to church to worship God will require a nicer set of clothes than going on a family picnic. "*Then David arose from the earth, and washed, and anointed himself, and changed his apparel, and came into the house of the LORD, and worshipped . . .*" —2 Samuel 12:20 But in any situation, be sure you are representing Christ by not wearing clothing that is immodest or so attractive that others' focus is on your *clothing* or *body* rather than your *countenance*. You should bathe regularly to be sure that you are fresh and clean.

When I go somewhere, I want people to see Jesus' light in my life. I do not want them to be attracted to my clothing. Instead, I want my clothing to be an indicator of what is inside. This should be our goal as we choose clothing to adorn our bodies. They should be God-honoring and "presentable" as we call it.

I remember one evening after I had been busy typing and preparing *Virtuous Daughters* for publication. It had taken me a long time, and I was tired. The time came for us to make copies, and as I walked in and waited for them, I began thinking about my outward appearance.

Yes, I was wearing modest clothes. In fact, the denim skirt was quite full, one plain color, and went almost to my ankles. The modest tee shirt was a solid color as well. However, both were quite casual—I believe the skirt had a small hole in the bottom of it, and the shirt might have had a stain from my wearing it "just around the house." Additionally, my hair was still in a careless braid from the night before.

Then I thought, "Am I representing Jesus? I come here every month for copies of a Christian newsletter, and I see the same woman each time. I really should devote more time to the care of my outward so that I am a better representation of my Lord."

As I said, the clothes were modest, yet they were not the clothes a daughter of the King wears when she is a representative of Him! ☺

The simple fact is that I should have put more time and thought into my outward before I left our home. I should have thought, "I am representing Jesus. I need to find a decent set of clothes that are appropriate for the occasion and representative of the King."

Since our family lives in the country and does a lot of work outside, we often wear casual, "work" clothes around the home and in the yard. A year or so ago, I noticed that it was difficult when we made an unexpected run to town for me to find decent, presentable clothes that were clean and pressed, as well as accessible. (Not that I don't own respectable clothes; I just have a hard time deciding what is best to wear in two or three minutes! ☺) My way to resolve this little dilemma was to choose a few sets of nice clothes that were casual but presentable. That way, I did not have to make any hasty decisions; I just grabbed the appropriate outfit, changed, and got in the van! ☺

As you go through daily life, you are representing Jesus Christ and His Word. You are representing Christianity, home schooling (if you home school), your parents, and most importantly, Jesus Christ our Lord. Be sure that your dress choice is apparel that the King is pleased with and that your parents delight in.

You are the King's daughter, and you should dress to represent and delight the King. You are adorning your outward for the *King*, not for the world or for the people you know. I know there have been times when I have dressed for the people I will be seeing. "I think I'll wear this because I look good in it and since I'll be seeing so and so . . ." This is not the attitude of the King's daughter! Every day when she dresses, she says, "Does this please my King? Is He honored when I wear this?" If the answer is yes, she wears it, regardless of who she will be seeing or what they might think. Never forget that "The outward ought to be a beautiful reflection of the inward." ♥

Dress Code

Many are fooled by the choice: "Skirts or pants?" They are looking at a very practical and achievable goal. That is not the question. I have seen some skirts that are quite worldly, and I think a girl would be better off clothed in modest pants than in a skirt that denotes a foolish attitude. The issue that every girl and woman needs to deal with is her heart's attitude and modesty.

". . . be clothed with humility: for God resisteth the proud, and giveth grace to the humble. Humble yourselves therefore under the mighty hand of God, that He may exalt you in due time."—1 Peter 5:5–6

Are you clothed in humility? Most women dress immodestly and worldly because they are prideful. Find your heart's attitude and dress by the guidelines of God's Word. One of the main ways you are *not* to dress is like the world. The world's dress is immodest and designed to be attractive to the outer appearance. Do not be deceived! *"And be not conformed to this world: but be ye transformed by the renewing of your mind, that ye may prove what is that good, and acceptable, and perfect, will of God."*—Romans 12:2

Another area women need to evaluate in their dress is whether it is *feminine*. "The woman shall not wear that which pertaineth unto a man, neither shall a man put on a woman's garment: for all that do so are abomination unto the Lord thy God."—Deuteronomy 22:5 If your clothes look like a man's clothes, something is wrong! Again, please use discernment and seek the Lord's direction and guidance.

Here is a dress code from God's Word that every woman and girl should earnestly work to follow:

> *"In like manner also*, that women adorn themselves in modest apparel, with shamefacedness and sobriety; not with braided hair, or gold, or pearls, or costly array; But (which becometh women professing godliness) with good works."   —1 Timothy 2:9–10

> *"Whose adorning* let it not be that outward adorning of plaiting the hair, and of wearing of gold, or of putting on of apparel; but let it be the hidden man of the heart, in that which is not corruptible, even the ornament of a meek and quiet spirit, which is in the sight of God of great price."   —1 Peter 3:3–4

Do you adorn yourself with good works? Do you possess a meek and quiet spirit? Do others know you for being kind, even though you may not wear expensive jewelry? Is it modest?

Several years ago, the girls in our family decided to start wearing skirts and dresses rather than pants or shorts. We were not vowing to "never wear pants again!," because the fact is, there were and still are times that we wear pants instead. However, we felt that the Lord was leading us to clothe our bodies in a more feminine fashion.

Truly the question is not whether to wear pants or a skirt. That is between you, your parents, and the Lord. Like one speaker said,

There are times when it might be more modest to wear a pair of pants than a skirt. Although I choose to wear dresses and skirts most of the time, if I am riding a horse, I know that pants would be more modest than a skirt.

I am not saying to wear either one, although I do feel that clothes with a feminine message are more modest and God-honoring for every woman or girl. However, there are times when it might be better to wear a pair of pants; use discernment and seek the Lord and your parents' guidance. Another option for girls is culottes. They are also known as "split skirts," because when worn they look like a skirt due to how full they are. They are usually a good length and considered modest. I have found culottes convenient when I am horseback riding, camping, playing outdoors, or when I want to wear something comfortable that is not too hot.

I have met so many girls and young women who are very friendly and kind, but their dress is awful! Modesty is not optional. There are simply no exceptions to it. God's Word highly exhorts women to dress themselves in a modest way. But knowing exactly what modest is can be a tough question for many. My suggestion is that you always "be safe rather than sorry," and look in the mirror at your clothes. Are there any "eye traps"? Is too much skin showing? Is the material "see-through"? Is it not too loose, but not too tight? One excellent question is, "What are people drawn to when I wear this?" If you are not sure, go ask one of your parents or mature siblings. All these little questions matter, and you should consider them before you wear a particular set of clothes. Again, you are dressing to please and glorify your King. Is He pleased with your dress selection? If so, then you have made a wise decision.

"But take heed lest by any means this liberty of yours become a stumblingblock to them that are weak."—*1 Corinthians 8:9* Again, we should always be sure that when someone looks at you, he or she is drawn to your countenance. Do not be a stumbling block to someone because your clothes are immodest, and they are drawn to something besides your face. This is not only displeasing to God, but it is not true love for those around you.

"*Do you love gaudy dresses* and useless ornaments? Remember that it is an evidence of an uncultivated taste and a vulgar and frivolous mind. If a woman is overloaded with gaudy ornaments and unsuitable dresses, they do not adorn her—she only bears about her person the badge of her inward deformity. Learn to understand the real beauty of simplicity. . . With . . . a mind absorbed by nobler things, you will despise the vain ornaments silly girls love. What innumerable evils have been the consequences of a foolish fondness for dress! To many it has been the cause of the first step in the wrong direction: it has been the entrance to that downward path which led them to a course of sin, a prison, or an early grave. . . Beware of the first appearance of such a taste! . . . Foster it not. Strive to check it as you would strive to check the first symptom of a fatal disease, the more insidious, because it appears slight and harmless at first."

—*The Basket of Flowers*

Make-Up

Some girls face the question whether to wear makeup or not, for others the decision comes naturally. Although I have chosen not to wear it at this time, I am definitely *not* in total disagreement with it! ☺ I have considered wearing it in the past, and may very well choose to wear it in the future. I believe that makeup is not wrong in most cases. If your mother wears makeup, and your grandmother does, and your great grandmother did . . . it may not even be a question for you! In my opinion, that is perfectly fine. Makeup adds a feminine touch, and many girls and women have fun with it.

The other side of makeup is, if you are so attached and dependent on it that you feel you cannot go to town or in public without it, then it has become too important in your life. A friend of mine told me that, while at retreats, she has often heard girls say while getting ready for bed, "Well, I guess I'll take off my face." One of the facts about makeup is right there in the name—it is a tool to "make up" something about you that does not even exist.

Is this what makeup is all about for you? Or is it a "girly" touch to add beauty to your face, and another way to direct others to your countenance? In some cases, makeup does just that, while in others, it does the exact opposite. Some girls wear a minimal amount of makeup that adds a natural look to cover blemishes, and they use a bit more on special occasions. Others I have met wear so much that it is a major distraction from their countenance.

While I do not think that makeup is wrong in itself, it can be a distraction, so you ought to, as always, use discretion and caution. A few other things to consider as you ponder whether you will wear makeup is the high expense of it, the time, and the number it can do on your skin! ☺ (I was told that the average girl "eats" six pounds of makeup in her lifetime! Ugh!)

Most of all, seek the Lord. If you are truly adorning your outward to please your King, you will ask Him what He wants you to do. Also, ask your parents. Just as a wife should adorn her outward to the glory and honor of her husband, so should you adorn your outward to the glory and honor of your parents and your Savior. Do they prefer you to wear makeup or not? Find out, and then joy in whatever way they think is nicest. Seek your King and follow your parents' guidance for best results! ☺

"The most important of all earthly things, are purity of heart and correctness of principle. Intellect, wealth, and beauty, are

of little value compared with goodness; and unless these gifts are accompanied with goodness, they serve to make the possessor unhappy within herself, and disliked by her companions." —The Girl's Own Book

Cover of Glory

"For if the woman be not covered, let her also be shorn: but if it be a shame for a woman to be shorn or shaven, let her be covered. Doth not even nature itself teach you, that, if a man have long hair, it is a shame unto him? But if a woman have long hair, it is a glory to her: for her hair is given her for a covering."
—1 Corinthians 11:6 & 14–15

One of the things that we are to adorn our bodies with is our hair. Sadly, some women of today are butchering all of their hair off, but years ago, that would have been a shame. It can take away the beauty and femininity of a woman. My sister is eight years old and has *never* had her haircut. I admire her for such a feat!

Let me encourage you to grow your hair out to a nice length, and you will be surprised how admired you will be by other girls and women. Hair is, like makeup, a fun and feminine thing to play with, but be sure that it *is* feminine. (Some women have hair *so* short that I would not know they were women by looking at it.)

What about getting a perm or highlight—the other things that you can do with your hair? To be quite candid, I believe the less chemicals and artificial sprays you put on your hair, the much healthier it is! A while back, I was frustrated with my hair because it always looked "frizzy" and "dull." When I mentioned this to another lady, she said, "Oh, you should get a perm! It's so easy—just put mousse in, brush it each day, and you're done! Besides, it looks really good."

This caught my interest. I have always felt I should not spend too much time trying to get my hair perfect. After omitting the cost as a factor, I thought maybe I should make it a consideration. Easy—pretty—quick. That is just for me! ☺

The more I thought about it, the more the Lord gently convicted me that I was being *prideful*. It was not just about spending less time with my hair. It was not just about being easy. It was as simple as the word pride. I dismissed the idea and yielded this desire to the Lord. "I'll be content with whatever, God. Please just help me to continue beautifying the inner."

To my surprise, it was not long after this that I really began to appreciate my hairstyle, and I am *so* glad I did not do any "major reconstruction" to it! I soon learned a couple of handy tips on keeping it frizz free, as well as how to allow it to have its natural curl without using the curling iron. I truly believe the Lord was trying to humble me and help me yield my rights to Him through this. I am awed at the way He works!

"But they that wait upon the LORD shall renew their strength; they shall mount up with wings as eagles; they shall run, and not be weary; and they shall walk, and not faint."
—Isaiah 40:31

This is not to say that we should not perm our hair, or do something similar to it. I certainly may consider that some day. But let's keep things in perspective as we seek to please our King!

Back to Beauty

We come back to beauty. What is it that God desires of us? It is natural and good for a girl to desire beauty in her life. But let her always keep in mind the Lord's dress code and to remember that she is adorning her outward to please the King—not the world, not her friends, not anyone else.

She can delight in putting on fancy clothes and dressing up; she can have fun playing with her hair, and coordinating colors. To enjoy making her outward beautiful is a pure and feminine thing to do. However, all of this should be done wisely and carefully. As my mother has always said, "Too much of anything is not good." As you do these things, watch the time and guard your heart. You are dressing to please your King.

"I have likened the daughter of Zion to a comely and delicate woman."
—Jeremiah 6:2 (The word *comely* here also means *dwelling at home*.)

The Secret of a Beautiful Life

"There once lived a young girl whose perfect grace of character was the wonder of those who knew her. She wore on her neck a gold locket which no one was ever allowed to open. One day, in a moment of unusual confidence, one of her companions was allowed to touch its spring and learn its secret. She saw written these words—"Whom having not seen, I love." That was the secret of her beautiful life.

—*Verses of Virtue*

Suggested Resources . . .

Books:
Verses of Virtue, compiled and edited by Elizabeth Beall Phillips
Daughters of Destiny, compiled and edited by Noelle Wheeler Goforth

---

An Extra Thought . . .

A Wordless Indicator
From *Virtuous Daughters,* By Sarah Hulin

. . . I have heard many girls say somewhat flippantly, "It's not what I wear that matters anyway! It's the heart." I agree, how important the condition of our heart truly is. We should never underestimate the need for maintaining its purity and godly focus. But, let's not swing so much on the pendulum to say that the outward doesn't matter . . . "For man looketh on the outward appearance, but the Lord looketh on the heart." (See 1 Samuel 16:7.) The thing is, man *does* look at the outward! You can't judge a book by its cover, right? True . . . but . . . if you walked into a bookstore and saw a book covered with gruesome monster-like figures, would you pick it out as something you think would be wholesome, edifying reading material? I hope not. The outward many, many times is an indicator of what is inside.

When you walk into the grocery store, and you interface with the lady at the meat counter, there are just a very few opportunities during your interfacing that can reflect your Savior. You've just a fragment of time, a glance and a few words (mostly about turkey or ham ☺). How can we achieve this task? A huge, wordless indicator that she will likely notice is that of your dress choice. The other things are so important too, like "yes ma'am," polite tones, kind words to siblings, and patience as you wait, and yes, perhaps on occasion you might actually be able to engage in a brief conversation on a spiritual thing or two. Just remember eyes are always watching, stranger, kinfolk, and friend alike. Remember that. Human eyes see and notice you from time to time, but more importantly God's [eyes] see and know every detail of your every moment!

Application...

"But be ye doers of the word, and not hearers only, deceiving your own selves."—James 1:22

Are you more concerned about outward or inward beauty? _____

Would you consider your dress representative of the King of all kings and Lord of all lords? _____ If not, what could you do to improve it?___
_____

Is your dress modest? _____ Why or why not? _____
_____

Are your parents pleased with your dress choice? _____
If not, what could you do to improve it? _____
_____

List two Scriptures that talk about beauty: _____
_____

Choose one of the following Scriptures to memorize and recite:
1 Peter 3:3–4   1 Peter 1:24
Psalm 39:11   2 Corinthians 4:16
Psalm 45:11, 13   Psalm 103:14–17

Recited to: _____ Date: _____

Choose one of the following activities to work on:
- Go through your wardrobe and take out any clothes you feel do not honor the King you represent.

- Choose a few casual but modest dresses specifically for running errands.

–Chapter x–
Becoming a Daughter of Purity

"Blessed are the pure in heart: for they shall see God."
—Matthew 5:8

Keeping My Heart Pure
From the World's Filth

Rose put the magazine she was reading on the floor. "This magazine is supposedly for Christian girls, but it sure contains a lot of things I don't feel are edifying me in my walk."

The world's filth is everywhere; how do we stay pure?

The World's Filth

"For the wisdom of this world is foolishness with God. For it is written, He taketh the wise in their own craftiness." —1 Corinthians 3:19

The world is filthy with sin. *". . . whosoever therefore will be a friend of the world is the enemy of God."*—James 4:4 Many young people are simply one step behind the world. Many young women have lost their purity because they are involved in the world's lusts.

It is sad that the pure, innocent girl with a godly heart is hard to be found! Nevertheless, that seems to be just the case in many of today's girls. Let it not be so in our lives! God has given us the responsibility of keeping our lives and hearts pure. *"For God hath not called us unto uncleanness, but unto holiness."*—1 Thessalonians 4:7

My parents have been careful to keep the hearts of their children pure from the world's filth. While under the protection of my parents, I do not have to know about every wicked and terrible thing that happens. I should praise the Lord for giving me godly parents who are wise in sheltering me.

The Bible says the pure are blessed because they will see God. God is pure. When a daughter is pure in all that she does, including her heart, she can better understand God and His ways. Anyone who is pure from the world is closer to God because God is not of this world. While there are things we must know, and others we cannot help knowing, there are certainly things we do not need to expose ourselves to.

"Love not the world, neither the things that are in the world. If any man love the world, the love of the Father is not in him. For all that is in the world, the lust of the flesh, and the lust of

the eyes, and the pride of life, is not of the Father, but is of the world. And the world passeth away, and the lust thereof: but he that doeth the will of God abideth for ever." —1 John 2:15–17

When we are a part of worldliness or even allow it into our lives by the TV, unwholesome books, or worldly friends, we have a greater struggle in making godly and right decisions. *"And the cares of this world, and the deceitfulness of riches, and the lusts of other things entering in, choke the word, and it becometh unfruitful."*—Mark 4:19 The world's filth is awful, and it comes in and takes away from the truth and goodness of God's Word in our hearts.

The Bible admonishes us to not only refrain from being a part of the world's filth, but we are to simply stay away from it. That is what purity is all about. It is taking the responsibility of living a life that is pleasing to God and not allowing the world to have an influence on your life. You may not think that by simply conversing with worldly friends or reading one article from an ungodly magazine you are being influenced, but you are much safer to stay away from it than to even take a glance. Take initiative! *"Dearly beloved, I beseech you as strangers and pilgrims, abstain from fleshly lusts, which war against the soul."*—1 Peter 2:11

What do we do when ungodly material "encircles" us? There are times when we certainly feel that way—standing at the checkout line amidst unwholesome magazines, driving down the road and approaching filthy billboards, going into the Christian bookstore and finding unedifying reading material . . . what do we do?!

If you see or hear something impure, simply do not dwell on that thought. If you can avoid seeing something that is not edifying (you can avoid reading the headlines on magazines at the checkout line), then avoid it! If you know there is a certain billboard on the street that is bad, do not look at it when you drive past! There is definitely some filth in our communities, but there are also ways to avoid it.

"For the grace of God that bringeth salvation hath appeared to all men, teaching us that, denying ungodliness and worldly lusts, we should live soberly, righteously, and godly, in this

present world; looking for that blessed hope, and the glorious appearing of the great God and our Saviour Jesus Christ; Who gave Himself for us, that He might redeem us from all iniquity, and purify unto Himself a peculiar people, zealous of good works." —Titus 2:11–14

Are you zealous of good works? Is your heart on fire for the Lord? Do you flee worldly lusts and keep even your heart and mind pure from the sins of the world? Do you live a life that is sober and righteous, pleasing, honoring and glorifying to Christ? Is your heart pure? *"Seeing ye have purified your souls in obeying the truth through the Spirit unto unfeigned love of the brethren, see that ye love one another with a pure heart fervently."*—1 Peter 1:22

Instead of Sin

Some young people fail to keep their *lives* pure. They want to "be in the circle," regardless of what the people in the circle are like or what they are doing. They do not live lives that please God. And yet there are still others who fail to keep their *hearts* pure. They do not try to "fit in," yet they still allow their mind to know of the world's lust, and they do not guard their hearts as they should. Guarding your heart is your responsibility, and you ought to take great care to fulfill that task.

"Flee also youthful lusts: but follow righteousness, faith, charity, peace, with them that call on the Lord out of a pure heart."—2 Timothy 2:2 Choose God's Word over sin! Choose to keep your heart pure from the world's sin, and Satan's ugly tricks. Stay away from worldly influences—do not allow yourself to be tempted. The more you expose yourself to the world's filth, the colder you become to sin.

Satan has a strong desire for you to give in, so he places many obstacles in your race. Do not give him the victory—defeat his evilness with the Word of God and prayer. A few months ago, several unwholesome billboards found their place on one of our main traveling roads. My parents were discouraged at this, but they refused to let Satan win the battle by exposing the sin to the minds of their children. Every time we would pass them, we took up our Bibles—the Sword of the Spirit—and read Scripture. What an excellent way to defeat Satan!

Finding Purity

So where do you go for purity in such an impure world? Even godly Christian books are now highlighting the lives of characters that possess worldly attitudes and struggle increasingly in sin. Some of the teens' books and novels severely lack high standard. If you cannot go to Christian stores for purity, if the churches have impurities, if people are not perfect (they are not!), then where do you go?

Where do we go when we cannot find righteousness and purity? The answer is the Lord. He is purity, righteousness, peace, love, and our only hope for tomorrow. He is the pure Lamb of God. *"But with the precious blood of Christ, as of a lamb without blemish and without spot."* —*1 Peter 1:19* If we seek God, He will show Himself to us. He will teach us and give us strength. *"And ye shall seek Me, and find Me, when ye shall search for Me with all your heart."*—*Jeremiah 29:13*

We must ask the Lord to forgive our sins and make us clean. He will purify our hearts if we ask Him to. *"Create in me a clean heart, O God; and renew a right spirit within me . . . The sacrifices of God are a broken spirit: a broken and a contrite heart, O God, Thou wilt not despise."*—*Psalm 51:10, 17*

"Have mercy upon me, O God, according to Thy lovingkindness: according unto the multitude of Thy tender mercies blot out my transgressions. Wash me thoroughly from mine iniquity, and cleanse me from my sin, for I acknowledge my transgressions: and my sin is ever before me. Against Thee, Thee only, have I sinned, and done this evil in Thy sight: that Thou mightest be justified when Thou speakest, and be clear when Thou judgest. Behold, I was shapen in iniquity; and in sin did my mother conceive me. Behold, Thou desirest truth in the inward parts: and in the hidden part Thou shalt make me to know wisdom. Purge me with hyssop, and I shall be clean: wash me, and I shall be whiter than snow. Make me to hear joy and gladness; that the bones which Thou hast broken may rejoice. Hide Thy face from my sins, and blot out all mine iniquities. Create in me a clean heart, O God; and renew a right spirit within me. Cast me not away from Thy presence; and take not Thy holy spirit from me. Restore unto me the joy of Thy salvation; and uphold me with Thy free spirit. Then will I teach transgressors Thy ways; and sinners shall be converted unto Thee. Deliver me

from bloodguiltiness, O God, Thou God of my salvation: and my tongue shall sing aloud of Thy righteousness. O Lord, open Thou my lips: and my mouth shall show forth Thy praise. For Thou desirest not sacrifice; else would I give it: Thou delightest not in burnt offering. The sacrifices of God are a broken spirit: a broken and a contrite heart, O God, Thou wilt not despise. Do good in Thy good pleasure unto Zion: build Thou the walls of Jerusalem. Then shalt Thou be pleased with the sacrifices of righteousness, with burnt offering and whole burnt offering: then shall they offer bullocks upon Thine alter."
—Psalm 51

God desires that we flee to Him when we cannot find purity because we can always find rest and peace in the Lord and in His Word. *"Every word of God is pure: He is a shield unto them that put their trust in Him."* —Proverbs 30:5 He also specifically instructs young people who are unsure what to do. *"Wherewithal shall a young man cleanse his way? By taking heed thereto according to Thy word."*—Psalm 119:9

By spending time in the Word of God, memorizing the Scriptures, and praying and seeking His will for our lives, you will come to know Him better and your life will be purer. You will be less aware of the world's filth because your eyes are on Jesus. Keep your eyes on Jesus, and you will always see purity!

Take a Stand!

"The wicked flee when no man pursueth: but the righteous are bold as a lion."
—Proverbs 28:1

I was ten as I sat at the kitchen table eating my breakfast. From daily habit, I had the package to the sweetened cereal sitting upright in front of me, and I read each word that covered the box. It was advertising some kind of toy for children, but when I saw it, I immediately realized it was not God-honoring. So as I finished my breakfast, I ran into the study, found a piece of notebook paper, and began to write.

Too bad I did not save a copy of my complaint letter. But I do remember it said something like "you are scaring little children with that 'meanie' stuffed animal. [The name of the toy included 'meanie.']

This does not please God! You should read the Bible, and find out the true way to happiness." Words like these filled an entire page, and I addressed an envelope, enclosed the letter, as well as a tract, and without hesitancy dropped it in the mailbox. In all honesty, I totally forgot about it.

Nevertheless, God honors even little children who try to make a difference. A few weeks later, I received a letter from a representative of Quaker Oats cereals. She apologized for having the inappropriate toy available to customers, and stated they would immediately stop the production of that package. She said to be sure to look at the shelves every time I went to the grocery store, because I would soon find new boxes! She also implied that she did not want to lose my business by enclosing a coupon and some stickers. ☺

I could not believe it! (Neither could my parents—they did not even know I had mailed the letter!) Every time we went to the grocery store, I searched the aisles for new boxes, and sure enough, they were there.

My point in telling you that was to encourage you—you can make a difference! This first "complaint" letter was the foundation for several more that I would write (but more kindly ☺). I did not always receive a response (more times I never heard back than I did), but still, I never knew if God was able to use that letter. If you see something that is hurting our society, heed the Spirit's leading and write to complain! Writing a letter is so easy and requires so little time—it could make a difference.

Ever so subtly, wickedness is entering our community, even our homes, through music, pictures, computer games, cereal boxes, and even toys! Our family in particular has had to be very careful about what computer games we allow in the home, as well as what toys. Several years ago, one of my toddler brothers received a cute little toy for his birthday. It taught science facts through bright animals and sounds. Without thinking about it, we handed it to him, but later realized that some of the words coming out were evolution—complete rejection of God's truth! My mother took a stand and complained.

Girls, whatever your age, take a stand! Make an effort to write, call, point out the wrongs, striving to make them right! Too often, we are deceived with the lie, "I am only one person"; but how many girls are saying that? If they all decided to make an effort, think of the difference that could be made in the world! You never know how God will use your testimony! Take a stand to fight the evil and defend the good! *"Be not overcome of evil, but overcome evil with good."*—Romans 12:21

A Heart of Pure Gold

"Lay hands suddenly on no man, neither be partaker of other men's sins: keep thyself pure." —1 Timothy 5:22

Have you ever received a piece of jewelry that was gold coated, but not true, pure gold? You might have been disappointed that it was not real metal. Perhaps you have been referred to as someone with a "heart of gold." But *is* it pure? Do you lead a life that pleases God?

The older a girl gets, the more she notices young men, and she sometimes begins to wonder who her future husband will be. Too often, she finds herself wrapped up in dreaming of the perfect young man, and she might even start thinking of names she already knows. Now remember, if young people did not have a longing to get married, families would never get started! However, the Lord does want us to keep our hearts pure and keep our sole focus on Him until the right timing. Let me encourage you to talk to your parents about this, and seek their counsel. They will give you wise advice in this area.

However, I would like to share just a little with you concerning this topic. Many of the women today who finally get married do not have hearts of pure gold. They have given their hearts away repeatedly, to different people, and all they have left for God's chosen life partner is a portion of their hearts. How sad! Not only that, but the redundancy of getting close, and then breaking away (dating, for example) is simply a preparation for divorce. It is a devastating situation.

I will assume that most of you are already committed to trusting your parents' counsel for a life partner. But how can you stay emotionally pure? The first step is to trust God for your future. There is no reason to sit wondering who God has in store to be your life partner. If you are constantly thinking about it, you will soon be discontent and discouraged. If you have a tendency to dream of a wonderful future, you will be disappointed when the time finally comes, because your expectations will have been too high. If a young woman cannot learn to be content in her present state, she will never be content—even when she has reached what she thought would make her happy (marriage, career, college, etc.) Do not try to look ahead at God's plans. Wait on His timing and use this time in your life for His glory.

I would also recommend that you avoid making close friendships with young men at this time in your life. It will not only help prevent thoughts toward certain people, but it will also encourage you to strengthen your relationships with your family and other friends. When God reveals to you and your family the life partner He has in store, there will be lots of time to become best friends with a young man! ☺ In the meantime, brothers make excellent close companions, and you can learn how to serve your father.

I do not mean that girls should not be courteous and friendly to boys. Of course young ladies should treat men with respect and kindness, but they ought to do it out of a pure heart. Do not be casual as you might be with your girlfriends; instead be formal and reserved in your actions and words. The truth is that a young man respects a young lady for her soberness, quietness, and discretion more than he does a girl who is casual and relaxed. *"Seeing ye have purified your souls in obeying the truth through the Spirit unto unfeigned love of the brethren, see that ye love one another with a pure heart fervently."*—1 Peter 1:22

"That they [aged women] may teach the young women to be sober, to love their husbands, to love their children, to be discreet, chaste . . . "—Titus 2:4–5 Keep a caution and guard. Your single years should not be wasted dreaming of the perfect courtship, husband, and home. You should take full advantage by using them to serve the Lord in various ways, and *prepare* to one day be that keeper at home. One night I remember thinking, "Will I really be the beautiful, godly, energetic, efficient, happy woman I dream of being in a few years? ☺ I am not going to make any difference just thinking about it—I need to *work* on it!" You see, we can think about it all we want to, but that does nothing to get us to the goal. It is like looking down a long road and thinking about how badly we need to walk it. Imagining the finish line, dreaming about how exciting it will be—but never starting down the road! We cannot, we *must* not, let this foolish wastefulness engulf us.

Instead of wondering who he is, or thinking about how wonderful he will be—it will only disappoint you when the time comes—work on becoming a woman of godliness who is content with her present situation. God honors those women and so do others! ☺ Enjoy these precious years with your family now; have fun with your siblings. Do not wish your time away.

Shelly Genovese, a young mother whose husband was killed in the terrorist bombing on 9-11-01 said the following,

"I used to try to rush life: 'I can't wait for it to be December. I can't wait till . . .' Now I wish I had spent more time enjoying every moment. Steve [her husband] always told me, 'Just enjoy every day. Don't wish it away.' He loved to live and he loved to work . . . I've lived here for five years and wasted five years of my life wishing I were back in Texas. Now all I wish is that I had my husband back. You realize how unimportant other things are. It really doesn't matter where you live, but how you live your life."

"And that ye study to be quiet, and to do your own business, and to work with your own hands, as we commanded you; that ye may walk honestly toward them that are without, and that ye may have lack of nothing."—1 Thessalonians 4:11–12 Sisters, enjoy the moments you have *now*. Do not lose the purity of your heart by always hoping for the perfect one. God will bring His best for you in the right time. For now, enjoy the life He has laid out before you, and strive to be a godlier woman.

A young woman who is pure in body, mind, and heart is a beautiful blessing! She will be able to give everything to her future husband instead of just what is "leftover." Make every effort to keep your heart pure; avoid young men who seem too casual or flippant with young ladies. And, although you ought to be kind and courteous to young men, remember to stay reserved and cautious. Do not even allow impure thoughts to enter your mind; instead, trust God for your future and life partner. He will bless you for your purity. "Let no man despise thy youth; but be thou an example of the believers, in word, in conversation, in charity, in spirit, in faith, in purity."—1 Timothy 4:12

Suggested Resources . . .

Books:
Least Said, Soonest Mended, by Agnes Giberne (This is an excellent book on not giving your heart away to those God did not intend you to.)
The Basket of Flowers, by J.H.St.A.
Clean Hands, by Isabella Alden

An Extra Thought . . .
Exercising Discernment in Reading
"But strong meat belongeth to them that are of full age, even those who by reason of use have their senses exercised to discern both good and evil."—Hebrews 5:14

Like most girls, I love to read! In my spare time, I can often be found cuddled up under a blanket in my bed reading a book. Reading is a wonderful skill and pastime. More so, it is an opportunity. To read a book is to gain knowledge, perhaps wisdom, and encouragement. For me, reading has also served as a writing tool. From different books, I am able to borrow phrases and writing styles I like. For centuries, people have loved to read—the illiterate were always looked at in sorrow. The more I've studied history, the more I realize that some of our wisest and most influential leaders were those who did a lot of reading.

But what kinds of books make a person great? The Bible, of course, is the best. However, not all books are godly or edifying reading material. Even in the Christian bookstores, we are surrounded by worldly sources. What sort of books are we to be reading? What about in the realm of Christian books or classic literature?

I believe that everything we do should be done in Jesus' name, and to His glory and honor. *"And whatsoever ye do in word or deed, do all in the name of the Lord Jesus, giving thanks to God and the Father by Him."* —*Colossians 3:1* Does this include reading? Definitely. Our reading material should be something that we would without hesitance hand to Jesus Himself. We must use discernment. Let me share with you how God has taught me this.

Even in "Christian" literature, we sometimes find material that is questionable or worldly. Here are some guidelines I have used to help me discern whether a book is edifying or not when I read. Of course, these are just suggestions; there are exceptions to the rule! ☺

If the main character is not a Christian, is he converted? There are few times when we are edified by reading about a person who does not love the Lord. Because we will probably have a tendency to long to be like the author-esteemed person, it is preferred that the character is a strong Christian, or at least a Christian successfully striving to a deeper relationship with the Lord.

Is the main character a somewhat glamorized naughty person throughout the book, and then in the last chapter spiritually improve? This is the number one flaw our family sees in children's Christian books. They give the reader nine chapters of bad, and one or one-half of the ending chapter of good. These are the type of books that, as you read, you are thinking, "Surely it will get better! Surely it will get better . . . " ☺ But it really never does. These books are not worthy of your time!

If the main character is undergoing circumstances, does he trust Jesus with them, "yielding his rights," and become satisfied, or is he only happy when everything works out the way **he** *wants it to?* I recently previewed a Christian fiction for my sister. It was about a twelve-year old girl in the 1800s. Meg, the main character, was a Christian and loved to draw. Her parents, however, did not approve of her drawing because they felt it was a waste of time. This was a struggle for her, and instead of giving her desires up to the Lord, she shared her battle with her best friend. Her friend encouraged her to draw anyway, so she did. Very often, she was secretly drawing in school or bed. She even took a secret trip to the art gallery at school. Does this sound like a godly example to follow?

In the end (the last two or three chapters), Meg is excited because she is able to learn more about drawing on a vacation she takes with her grandmother. She becomes "changed" into a godlier and happier person when her parents give her permission to draw on a regular basis after the vacation. I thought about the plot as I did dishes—wouldn't it have been better if the character had given up her desires to the Lord and trusted Him? Then, when she was *content* in *trusting the Lord*, maybe she could have been rewarded for her unselfish attitude by being allowed to draw—a double blessing. Look out for subtle things like this; it was a Christian book, and so was the main character, but she did not display a Christian attitude. She was not happy until she "won" the battle she was so desperately fighting.

Look for good examples to learn from rather than negative ones. I have seen many books and children's devotionals that give negative examples and the author expects a young mind to learn from it! They anticipate that the reader will see the wrong and long to do the good. But very often this is not the case. If you are like me, you long to emulate the most admired and loved character! ☺ I remember reading a book several years ago about a daughter who was a constant servant in helping her mother keep house. She made many of the family meals and loved to sew. When I set down the book, I went straight to the kitchen, looked at the clock, and cheerfully made lunch! ☺

Although I have never read an "Elsie Dinsmore" book myself, and therefore cannot recommend them, it is my understanding that Martha Finley did an excellent job at maintaining a positive example of a godly girl for the readers to follow. I have heard many comments like, "She's perfect; it's too hard to learn from her." I understand, and would certainly agree that a character should not be elevated as *perfect* because only Christ is truly perfect. Nevertheless, if the character is truly striving to be like Christ, yet humble, she will definitely be a good example to read about!

Does the work completely contradict everything you believe? In school, some of my literature is about the Greek gods or atheistic legends. To read this would be like reading a book about the theories of evolution. Why fill your mind with things that you totally reject?

What is the author's background? This is valuable information when discerning whether a book will be good or not. As my mother always says, an author's beliefs, feelings, convictions, and life will come out in his writings—even if it's a story. Before reading a book that you are unsure about, including classics, research the author's life a bit.

In school I read a short story titled "To Build a Fire," by Jack London. It was about a man and his dog traveling through snow and running into many predicaments. Although he never directly said this, I noticed that the author was exalting the dog above the man, because in every problem they had, the dog was thinking of the right thing to do, and the man's complete imprudence kept him from making appropriate decisions. The man continuously made life-threatening mistakes, while the dog was (in its "mind") thinking of how to save their lives. In the end, the man froze to death, and the dog successfully made it to the camp they were headed to.

It didn't hit me much until I read the author information section. Jack London was highly influenced by the works and beliefs of Charles Darwin, Karl Marx, and Nietzsche. London himself was a socialist! It also stated that he lived dangerously and furiously, dying at the age of forty. By knowing the author's background, I was able to assume that his works, even though popular, are probably something I do not want to read because what he believed will no doubt come out in his writings in a subtle way.

Seek the Lord to help you discern between good and bad in your books. Look for the character traits you know God wants to see in your life. If you read a story and see undesirable qualities, note that. In grammar, I do several critical book reviews a year. The goal is to get a *critical* idea of what the book was about. I have to discern whether the author used good writing skills, whether his writing was accurate, and whether it was overall good reading material. You don't have to do a written report on every book you read, but do a mental critical review. The books you read will likely influence you, and you want it to be for the good.

Never forget that parents are excellent counselors in the area of reading. They are older and wiser, and will give thorough advice.

Lastly, use *Philippians 4:8* as an overall guideline when you read. *"Finally, brethren, whatsoever things are true, whatsoever things are honest, whatsoever things are just, whatsoever things are pure, whatsoever things are lovely, whatsoever things are of good report; if there be any virtue, and if there be any praise, think on these things."* Whatever we read will be what we dwell on—what we think about. By reading things that are in line with this verse, you are reading good literature! Happy reading!

Application...

"But be ye doers of the word, and not hearers only, deceiving your own selves."—James 1:22

Could people label you as having a pure heart? Why or why not? _____
_____

What does the Scripture "Blessed are the pure in heart: for they shall see God" (Matt. 5:8) mean? _____
_____

What impure things (books, TV shows, magazines, etc.) could you dispose of? _____
_____

List two Scriptures that speak of purity: _____
_____

Choose one of the following Scriptures to memorize and recite:

1 Timothy 4:12　　　　　　　Titus 2:12
1 John 2:15–17　　　　　　　Matthew 5:8
1 Thessalonians 4:7　　　　　Mark 4:19

Recited to: _____ Date: _____

Choose one of the following activities to work on:

- Go through your things and dispose of anything worldly that you do not think Jesus would be pleased with. Is there anything you would not want Him to see? It better go out the window! ☺

- Write an essay about what it means to have a pure heart.

–Chapter XI–
Becoming a Daughter of the Home

"That they [aged women] may teach the young women to be sober, to love their husbands, to love their children. To be discreet, chaste, keepers at home, good, obedient to their own husbands, that the word of God be not blasphemed."—Titus 2:4–5

Serving in the Home
As Preparation to be a Future
Keeper at Home Myself

"**What** did you say your plans after graduation are?" the woman asked fifteen-year old Sarah.

"Well," she swallowed hard, Why is it always so hard to say this? "I plan to continue helping my mother in the home so that I will be better equipped when God calls me to be a helpmeet and keeper of my own home someday."

Most people do not understand why a girl should stay in the home these days. She does not want recognition? What does it mean to be a **daughter of the home**?

Home Sweet Home

Home is so sweet. Of course there are times when we need to "get out of the house," but no other place can offer the comfort and protection of a loving home. After a long day of shopping and running errands, I always feel happy and encouraged to walk in the door of my sweet home.

Home educators get to spend their entire day in the home! Some may think of that as stressful, and it can be at times, but it is one of the greatest joys in the world. I have found that in our family's home walls, I have learned some of my greatest lessons, had my greatest fun, built my strongest friendships, and grown closer to the Lord than I ever would have any other place.

Every girl should love her home. A woman's place and greatest opportunity for God to use her is in her home. Willingly and cheerfully, daughters should learn to work alongside their mothers to make their house a home. They should diligently make it the place their family longs to be after a long or tiresome day.

Making a home sweet is more than decorations or food on the table three times a day. It is the love of Christ and the Word of God. Do the family members exhibit a love for their Lord? Is the home built on the Holy Bible? Is Jesus Christ ever-present? Are the mother and sisters meek and quiet, loving and encouraging? These are some things that make a house a sweet home.

What a Home Ought to Be

"A home ought to be a place of rest and comfort, love and peace. One should be able to come to his home and find outstretched arms and warm shelter. His home should be the place where he can share his burdens, and be encouraged. A home ought to be the place one looks forward to after a difficult day. May every home be praised in this way, 'There's no place like home!'"

—Tiffany Schlichter

A Woman's High Calling

"She looketh well to the ways of her household, and eateth not the bread of idleness."—Proverbs 31:27

Many of today's women are blinded to their responsibilities. They fail to realize that their greatest place is in the home, and they can fulfill their calling best by serving their husband and children. God first ordained man and woman's callings in Genesis—man is to be the breadwinner for the family, while woman is to bear and raise children.

Women need to realize that they do not have to and should not be taking on two responsibilities. By working outside of the home, they are neglecting their family. God knew who could care for and raise up children for Him best—it was not daycare, or the school, not even the father. It is the mother.

When women started leaving the home, our country began to fall apart. The strong men and women who were lovingly and wisely being raised are now turning to folly. There is no mystery to solve—women left the home and were no longer guiding the hearts of their children to the Lord and His ways.

"Persuading thousands of young mothers to go out to work and to abandon the care of their children to others is one of the most disastrous things at the present time. What is it going to profit the nation, if we gain the dollars—or even the whole world—but lose the souls of our children? Now that the State is lifting so much responsibility from parents, the bond of love between parents and their

children is in danger of being loosened. It is when the mothers of the nation begin to fail in their duty to their children that religion disappears, moral standards fail, and the nation begins to go down."

—Enid Blyton

Praise the Lord for the women who have been strong in Him and who have made the decision to stay in their home and serve their families. There is hope for the generation to come because mothers are once again coming into their homes. Let us pray for these mothers and their children that God will continue to work in their hearts and lives to conform them to His image.

Girls, never forget that woman's highest calling is homemaker. She runs the house, she sees to the family's needs, she supports and completes her husband's vision, and she raises children who can one day be soldiers for the Lord's army. I love this passage from the excellent fiction *Mother*:

> "I know *what makes you so different* from other women . . . It's having that wonderful mother! . . . She's one woman in a million. It's something to thank God for, a mother like that . . . I've been wondering what she gets out of it; but I think I've found it out. This morning, thinking what her life is, I couldn't see what repaid her, do you see?
>
> "What made up to her for the unending effort and sacrifice, the pouring out of love and sympathy and help—year after year after year . . .
>
> " . . . These days, when women just serenely ignore the question of children, or at most, as a special concession, bring up one or two— just the one or two whose expenses can be comfortably met!—there's something magnificent in a woman like your mother, who begins eight destinies instead of one! She doesn't strain and chafe to express herself through the medium of poetry or music or the stage, but she puts her whole splendid philosophy into her nursery . . . Responsibility—that's what these other women are afraid of! But it seems to me there's no responsibility like that of decreeing that young lives simply shall not be. Why, what good is learning, or elegance of manner, or painfully

acquired fitness of speech and taste and point of view, if you are not going to distil it into the growing plants, the only real hope we have in the world? . . . There's a higher tribunal than the social tribunal of this world, after all . . ."

The virtuous woman we find in Proverbs 31 is noted for her service to her husband and children—the people who make up her home. She diligently and lovingly trains her children and serves her husband. She runs the household by providing food and clothing. She sets a godly example by her wise words and willing hands. She is praised for seeing that the needs of her home and family are met.

Sisters, the time will come when God calls us to motherhood. We cannot, we *must not,* forsake our duty. It is not just a calling; it is God's design for women. To train the hearts of your children and meet the needs of your husband will one day be your only "job," so to speak. It is an important one. The Bible says that women are to be keepers *at* home—all these things—that the *Word of God is not blasphemed.* Do not think that you will one day be married, have kids, and find a second outside job. You will have to pour your *whole life* into your family, or it will likely crumble. It will be a commitment. It will be a challenge. It will be different. But it is and always will be God's way, it is the only way; and it works!

"There is nothing which brings more fulfillment in the life of a woman than being the helpmeet that God designed and created her to be. God alone knows what will bring a woman happiness. We cannot glorify God in any other role than the one for which we were created." —Susan Zakula, in *The Joy of Womanhood*

"I have likened the daughter of Zion to a comely and delicate woman." —Jeremiah 6:2 The word *comely* also means *dwelling at home.* A keeper at home is one who dwells in her home to meet the needs of the home and the people in it. A keeper of the home—a wife and mother—is a beautiful woman.

Why Motherhood?

Obviously, we cannot predict the future. We do not know what it holds—we only know Who holds it—the Almighty God. Any of us could be single for the rest of our lives, or maybe even married but never having children. This is in the hands of the Lord, and we trust Him with yesterday, today, tomorrow, and every day ahead.

However, I believe few of us will be called to a life of single womanhood, without a family. God's master plan is that " . . . *the younger women marry, bear children, guide the house . . .* "—1 Timothy 5:14 We need to accept and embrace this calling! Be excited about the trust God has put in you to some day bring new life into the world and to train these little ones to be enduring soldiers of Jesus Christ!

Today, there is little value placed on life. Not only is having children looked down upon, but some parents murder their babies before they are even born! We cannot be influenced by the evil thinking in this culture. We must realize that it is up to us to bring another generation of godly men and women to our dying world.

Several months back, my mother read from the local newspaper an article by a liberal writer about how the conservatives are beginning to "outdo" many of the liberals in population. Because godly families have chosen to allow the Lord to bless them with many children, they are raising up a strong and large generation to fight this battle. Praise the Lord!

You may see being a mother as a menial task, something undesirable and not "good enough." I, too, have had these thoughts. Should I not do something more exciting with my life and make a huge difference? The truth is, however, I am *one* person. I can only make so much difference. Suppose in the future, God blesses me with a husband and children. How much *more* difference can I make if I bring more lives into the world, and train them to be devoted followers of Jesus Christ? Then there are my children's' children, and their children. The ripple goes farther than we think.

Even in the Christian society, we do not hear it as much—the importance of wifehood and motherhood. In fact, even in the Christian *home school* environment this is not always accepted. I still remember the look on one home schooling mother's face. She had been talking to me about the publication of my first book, asking if I planned to get a degree in journalism or some other writing degree, or if I was going to take up writing as a permanent career.

I kindly explained to her that I definitely wanted to improve my skill and possibly write more books in the future, but felt that God was mainly calling me to be a keeper at home. She looked at me surprised and a little confused. I would expect that with a woman who had a career and sent her children off to school, but with a woman who is committed to her home and family? I was confused now too.

Girls, disregard these little embarrassing responses; press on in what you know is right! Keep running the race for Jesus Christ, and continue your hope and vision for someday raising *soldiers for Him!* Let me close this challenge with an excerpt from something I wrote:

"*The world will tell you* to despise housekeeping and reject children. That is today's attitude. Our world—our country even—does not put a high value on life. Face it. You will be told that children are nuisances and that if you want kids, no more than one or two. Do not listen, do not heed, Satan's lies! He will try to deceive you, but you must not follow. Instead, embrace God's design and prove that motherhood is worth all the efforts. Being a mother is raising the next generation. Prove that children are a blessing and they are help, not hindrance. Do not just believe it, do not just preach it, and do not just practice it listlessly. Look forward to the day when you can pursue and prove what you know is God's design, what you know is right, and what you know works.

"Especially as you get older, people will ask, 'What do you want to do with your life?' You may get tired of the surprised and disappointed looks on their faces when you say you would like to be a keeper at home and some day raise children for the Lord. People think, 'Why? She's going to waste her life like that?!'

"I read a poem that says 'the hand that rocks the cradle is the hand that rules the world.' Never think your future 'job' as a mother is insignificant. What if Mrs. Washington had chosen to put herself in the spotlight and never start a family? What if my mother had chosen to stop at one child? What if my grandmother had chosen to stop at one? None of us (my mother, siblings, aunt, cousins, or me) would even be here! What if Mary had forsaken her duty as a mother? What if she had not cared, or had tried to put herself first?

"I think God wants women to look to Mary much more than we do. Nothing else in this world's history is more important than the coming of Jesus Christ. And how did He get here? Through a young woman who was willing to be a mother and raise a child. No other duty in the world has been more important.

"We cannot see the future. But we can hope and pray that some day we will have the honor and privilege of mothering future soldiers for Christ. I hope you do the same. I am sure you will. ☺"

A Daughter's Hope & Vision

"Blessed is the man that trusteth in the LORD, and whose hope the LORD is."
—*Jeremiah 17:7*

Every girl has hope. She has hope to someday be a special and admired person. She hopes to one day fulfill the job God has in store for her. To be a girl is to hope.

Praise God for daughters who hope in the name of the Lord for good and righteous things! *"The hope of the righteous shall be gladness: but the expectation of the wicked shall perish."*—*Proverbs 10:28*

Ever since I can remember, friends and I have discussed "what we want to do when we grow up." It is always an interesting thing to share. My friends would tell me they wanted to be doctors, gymnasts, veterinarians, and many other admired business people. But blessed be the girl who says with hope and vision that she longs to one day serve the Lord as a godly wife and mother—a keeper of the home. God will surely use this daughter for His glory.

The norm today is for a girl to graduate with plans for college and a career. If she does get married, she remembers that keeping house and raising few if any children is only second to her job and spotlight. The Bible instructs women differently:

> "But speak thou the things which become sound doctrine: that the aged men be sober, grave, temperate, sound in faith, in charity, in patience. The aged women likewise, that they be in behavior as becometh holiness, not false accusers, not given to much wine, teachers of good things; that they may teach the young women to be sober, to love their husbands, to love their children, to be discreet, chaste, keepers at home, good, obedient to their own husbands, that the word of God be not blasphemed." —Titus 2:1–5

D. L. Moody once affirmed "All that I have ever accomplished in my life I owe to my mother." Many women will testify that being a wife and mother is one of the greatest joys in the world. The women who put their time, effort, and heart into such a task are sometimes unnoticed and unrecognized by outsiders, but God will reward them for their labor. One day she will see the fruit of her labor as her children do great things for God. She will see that her service has eternal riches, while the service of many others is only temporarily praised.

My mother puts it this way:

> "... *Let's not forget* those in our own home. It's easier sometimes to help those outside our home, because we may get more recognition for it. But what does the Bible say about this? 'Not with eye service, as men pleasers; but as the servants of Christ, doing the will of God from the heart.'—Ephesians 6:6 If you have a habit of loving and serving those in your own home, how easy it will be to serve those outside of your home. And the solid relationships you will build with your family will last a lifetime, unlike most friendships that change over time. Everything you learn for your future, you are learning now in your own home. Praise God for your family!"
>
> —Mrs. Cheryl Schlichter, in *Virtuous Daughters*

"*Where there is no vision, the people perish: but he that keepeth the law, happy is he.*"—*Proverbs 29:18* God is calling girls to have a vision for tomorrow—for girls to hope in being a keeper at home in the future. You will reap eternal benefits if you serve the people nearest you—your own family.

At one time, small girls had vision and hope of one day being homemakers. They served alongside their mothers and learned everything they could about keeping a house. The daughters assisted their mothers in caring for the children and cooking dinner that they may be better equipped when the time came for them to be keepers at home as well.

> "*When a woman says* she is a housewife she should say it with the utmost pride, for there is nothing higher on the planet to which she could aspire."
> —John Seymour, *The Forgotten Arts and Crafts*

The same principle can grip our girls today. Do you lack hope and vision for being a homemaker? Serve with your mother and ask her the joys of being a keeper of the home. Learn how to care for a household, how to encourage your father and brothers, how to train the small children. You will be encouraged and excited about serving God in this mighty way.

I'd Rather

Meredith Gray

I'd rather be a mother
Than anyone on earth,
Bringing up a child or two
Of unpretentious birth.

I'd rather tuck a little child
All safe and sound in bed—
Than twine a chain of diamonds
About my foolish head.

> *I'd rather wash a smudgy face*
> *With round, bright baby eyes—*
> *Than paint the pageantry of fame,*
> *Or walk among the wise.*

A Strong Home

What is the secret to making a house a strong home for the family? The key is the Rock on which you build it—Jesus Christ. Is the Lord a part of your every day conversation and your time together? Is His Word read and studied as a family and individually on a regular basis? Do not only teach God's Word, but also *live* it to make it a part of your family. A home and family that is built on these things will be strong.

Have you ever noticed that the upper half of the panels on most doors represents a cross? I used to think this was mere coincidence, but it was not. The original architects and designers did this so that when one enters a room, he will remember Christ. This should be an ongoing reminder to keep His Word alive in our hearts and homes.

As you go through each day, lovingly instruct your siblings in doing what is right. Remind your mother that God is using her in your life, and encourage your father in his diligent endeavors to support the family. These things knit a family together.

Never think that only your mother makes the home, but realize that you are a part of this, too. I have friends who are completely responsible for the family meals in their home, and they do it with a joyful and willing heart. They accept their task with love, and serve the family in a special way.

In spite of the constant call for a woman to serve outside of the home, God calls us in the home. This is one of the main ingredients to a strong home. The following is firm; nevertheless, it is truth and needs to be stated:

> *"If you refuse to obey* God's Word, His precepts, His plan for your life—you are like Eve. You think God has lied to you, and you believe Satan rather than God. You may think a career will bring more ful-

fillment instead of being satisfied by being a helpmeet and mother, but you will find out like Eve, that it is foolish to aspire to things outside of God's plan for you. The evil one even deceives Christian women by enticing them to leave their homes for the Christian workforce or some good-sounding cause. However, this leaving of our homes still results in our families being abandoned in many ways."

—Susan Zakula, in *The Joy of Womanhood*

By being a delightful daughter and loving sister, you have a role in making your house a home. Your family will honor and love you if you just put some effort into strengthening the relationships and serving the household. God blesses a willing servant, who is content and happy with *any* task He gives her!

Service in the Home

Besides helping keep the house running and in order, what else does a daughter do to make the house one of strength and grace? She is quick to serve and honor her parents. She longs to help complete their vision and goal.

The greatest place any woman has ever served is in the walls of her home. Grandmothers, mothers, and daughters alike have been serving their families, and God has used them mightily for Him. He designed a woman to be a helpmeet to her husband, and she best fulfills her life purpose in doing so.

What are young daughters to be doing? God designed daughters to work alongside their mothers to learn and benefit from them all they can, so that when the daughter does get married, she is capable of her duties, and she understands her job. In addition to learning, however, she must serve her parents. She can be a helper in their endeavors.

Represent your parents as you go places, and ask them how you can complete their vision. They may assign you a task that can be your own responsibility that is a part of their ministry. Daughters of missionaries can relate to this well and have much experience in helping their parents in their ministry. Any girl can do it; just find out how.

I am always impressed with young women who have chosen to joyfully serve and benefit their parents. Girls who concern themselves with "But I want to be recognized, and I can't be if all I do is serve my parents," are not preparing for marriage and a family. On the contrary, a young lady who says, "I am happy to serve my father and mother. What can I do for you, Mom and Dad?" will make a wonderful homemaker and helpmeet!

> *"Home*, with all its prohibitions and opportunities to die daily" offered training far greater than any Bible school curriculum.
>
> —Amy Carmichael, missionary to India

The Best Place to Be

I read a short story titled "If I Live till Sundown," by Henry Woodfin Grady. It was about a wounded soldier left on the battlefield to die. At first his only hope was the promise of a passing surgeon, "If he but lives till sundown, he will get well." But that was not enough to keep him strong and determined as he lay on the ground. He needed a hope with more foundation and meaning, and he thought of his home,

> "... *It* [*the sun*] *sloped down* its slow descent, and his life was ebbing away and his heart was faltering, and he needed stronger stimulants to make him stand the struggle until the end of the day had come. He thought of his far-off home, the blessed house resting in tranquil peace with the roses climbing to the door, and the trees whispering to its windows, and dozing in the sunshine, the orchard, and the little brook running like a silver thread through the forest.
>
> "'If I live till sundown, I shall see it again. I shall walk down the shady lane; I shall open the battered gate, and the mocking-bird will call to me from the orchard, and I shall drink again at the old mossy spring.'
>
> "And he thought of the wife who had come from the neighboring farmhouse and put her hand shyly in his, and brought sweetness to his life and light to his home.
>
> " 'If I live till sundown, I shall look once more into her deep and

loving eyes, and press her brown head once more to my aching breast.'

"And he thought of the old father, patient in prayer, bending lower and lower every day under his load of sorrow of old age.

" 'If I but live till sundown, I shall see him again and wind my strong arm about his feeble body, and his hands shall rest upon my head, while the unspeakable healing of his blessing falls into my heart.'

"And he thought of his little children that clambered on his knees and tangled their little hands into his heartstrings, making to him so much music as the world shall not equal . . .

" 'If I live till sundown, they shall again find my parched lips with their warm mouths, and their little fingers shall run once more over my face.'

"And he then thought of his old mother, who gathered these little children about her, and breathed her old heart afresh in their brightness and attuned her old lips anew to their prattle, that she might live till her big boy came home.

" 'If I live till sundown, I shall see her again, and I will rest my head at my old place on her knees, and weep away all my memory of this desolate night.' "

The family of this man had made his house a home. He would rather be in his home than anywhere else. Have you made your house such a wonderful place to be that it is home to your family, and they long to be there? *"Better is a dinner of herbs where love is, than a stalled ox and hatred therewith."*—*Proverbs 15:17*

Where is the best place to be? Where do you prefer? What about your siblings? Your parents? If the answer is home, then God is working through your life, and He will continue. Make home and family the best place to be by your joyful, cheerful countenance, and willing, loving heart. God will use you in ways you cannot even imagine if your heart is in your home!

Chapter Eleven—Becoming a Daughter of the Home ☙

"*Examine yourself*. If you were left alone among strangers, do you possess any useful qualities or talents which would make them wish to keep you with them? Can you be of any use? Are you leading a useful life? or are you so wholly selfish and useless, that if you went away, no one would regret you—if you died, no one would miss you?"
—*The Basket of Flowers*, by J. H. St. A.

Suggested Resources . . .

Books:
Homemaking, by J.R. Miller
Keepers at Home, by Susan Zakula
Wives of the Signers, foreword by David Barton
Mother, by Kathleen Norris
The Basket of Flowers, by J.H.St.A.

An Extra Thought . . .

Scheduling Tips

The Bible says *"Let all things be done decently and in order."—1 Corinthians 14:40* I agree! There are certainly days when I feel unproductive, and I realize what has gone wrong . . . I have followed no schedule!

In order for a day to go smoothly and something to get done, we must have a plan—a schedule. A few things that I am working on are . . .

🕐 **Rise early!** I'll have to admit that I struggle in this area more than the others. ☺ However, I have no excuse! Getting up on time is a must to a workable schedule. In our home, 6:00 is the preferred time, and a couple hours later for the little ones. We start school at 7:00, which leaves one hour for quiet time, breakfast, and anything else we need to do while it's still quiet. Sometimes this hour seems short, but for our family it has worked well.

For me, the time I get up seems to decide how the rest of my day will go. When I get up on time, I feel fresh, motivated, and get a lot accomplished. Days that I sleep in, however, I usually feel lazy, and my day seems to fly away. I guess I can learn from the Proverbs 31 woman: *"She riseth also while it is yet night, and giveth meat to her household, and a portion to her maidens."—Proverbs 31:15*

🕐 **Keep a goal!** Sometimes when I am making my journal entry at night, I like to write everything I want to accomplish the next day. This gives me a goal for the next day and helps me to stay focused. Days when I do not have any goals, I usually end up wasting a lot of time.

🕐 **Make a schedule!** One of the best things to do to plan your day is to make a schedule. Take a blank piece of paper and write out the day in an hour-by-hour format. Fill in the spaces with the things that need to be done, as well as things you would like to get done. It's amazing how much extra time there is when we schedule activities by the hour!

🕐 **Get everything!** When you write out a schedule, do not just plan out the highlights for the day, like piano lessons or meetings. Make a space for the necessary, every-day things, too, like grooming, Bible study, school, chores, etc.

🕐 **Paste it up!** Once you've drawn out a schedule, paste it in your room so you can have it to review. You want to make it a part of your daily focus. Also, don't forget to have your parents approve of it. ☺

🕐 **Prioritize!** Very often, a stressful day is due to wrong prioritizing. Remember to keep your priorities straight: first, God; second, family; third, others; fourth, you. This is a must!

Learn to keep a schedule now, and it will be a blessing to you every day of your life! Happy scheduling!

Application...

"But be ye doers of the word, and not hearers only, deceiving your own selves."—James 1:22

Is the majority of your time spent in your home, or somewhere else? Is your heart truly in your home? _____

Do you cheerfully serve alongside your parents, helping to complete their vision and work in their ministry? Do you enjoy serving them? _____

What do you want to do with your life when you are grown? _____

Will you be content to serve as only a wife and mother when you are married? How can you begin preparing for that now? _____

List two Scriptures that suggest the importance of being a keeper at home: _____

Choose one of the following Scriptures to memorize and recite:

Titus 2:1–5   *Proverbs 31:10–31*
Jeremiah 17:7   *Proverbs 10:28*

Recited to: _____ Date: _____

Choose one of the following activities to work on:
- Choose a homemaking skill to learn and utilize.

- Be responsible for the family dinners for one week.

–Chapter XII–
Becoming a Daughter of Service

"Be kindly affectioned one to another with brotherly love; in honour preferring one another; not slothful in business; fervent in spirit; serving the Lord." —Romans 12:10–11

Serving the Lord
In Whatever Ways He Calls

Julia knows she should be a servant of the Lord. She already does a lot of work, but is occasionally told she does not have the right attitude. She longs to be the "good and faithful" servant the Bible speaks of in Matthew 25.

Every girl is to be a servant, wherever or whenever that is. How should she serve?

A Willing Heart

"But now, O LORD, Thou art our Father; we are the clay, and Thou our Potter; and we all are the work of Thy hand."—Isaiah 64:8

Have you ever worked with clay? If so, you can probably recall that it is a sticky process, but rewarding at that. The time spent may seem unprofitable at the moment (it did for me!☺), but the lessons to be learned are worth every minute.

I was about six or seven years old the first time I put my hand to pottery. My grandmother had bought a children's clay pottery set, and she was demonstrating how to make a project while allowing me to participate. We would wet the clay and then shape it to look right. Sometimes we had to fix it in little places, and we had to work with it for a good while to produce the desired effect. We were the designers of this project.

Many girls do not realize that God is molding them into His image day by day. At times, we girls can be stubborn to God's work in our lives. There are times when I do not see *why* He is doing something, so I fail to trust Him with that situation. This is not the attitude of a faithful servant.

When I yield myself to the will of the Father, I must ask Him to mold me as He desires, and He will use me. Clay that is hard as a rock cannot be used unless it is wet, right? So a girl who is obstinate to God's will cannot be used for His glory unless she allows Him to cleanse her from her sins, and she yields her life to Him. When she does this, the work of God has begun in her heart.

We need to put *our* desires aside and ask the Lord to use us in the way that would please Him best. This is the starting point for Him to use us in more ways than conceivable. He is able to work in my life when I am like clay that is flexible to the plans of the potter. Yet my life has much more purpose and ability than a piece of mere clay, and my life is in the hands of the loving and omniscient Father rather than a foolish and simple human.

If you ever have the opportunity to either work with clay or watch the process, I highly recommend it! Perhaps the most vivid memory I have of this is from a couple of years ago when my siblings and I were able to watch a professional potter at work. It was the most amazing thing! He could take a lump of clay that was ugly and looked worthless, and make it into something beautiful and useful. The time it took for him to make something, and the way it came out, however, all depended on the flexibility of the clay. If it was obstinate, he would be working on it for several minutes, but nothing seemed to go right. He would then throw the clay to the side. The flexible clay, however, became beautiful pieces of pottery that honored and glorified the potter.

What kind of "clay" are you? Right now you may feel useless, but yield to God's will and be willing to do whatever He sets before you. He will use you in ways you cannot imagine. A servant does not argue orders; she does not ask for bigger or smaller jobs. She is content with the task she is given, and is faithful to complete it in a diligent manner.

Handmaid of the Lord

"Behold the handmaid of the Lord; be it unto me according to Thy word . . ."
—Luke 1:38

I have always loved that phrase, "handmaid of the Lord." It holds so much meaning and such a beautiful, willing heart! There are times when I am given a task from my parents (ultimately from the Lord), and I feel it is insignificant or unimportant. Why this? Could I not have received something bigger?

The truth is that I should be *honored* to have the *privilege* of serving my Lord and parents. Jesus' mother Mary held this attitude. Think about the words of gratefulness and joy she spoke when she was informed that she would be mother to the Savior of the world:

"... *Behold the handmaid* of the Lord; be it unto me according to Thy word . . . My soul doth magnify the Lord, and my spirit hath rejoiced in God my Savior. For He hath regarded the low estate of His handmaiden: for, behold, from henceforth all generations shall call me blessed. For He that is mighty hath done to me great things; and holy is His name. And His mercy is on them that fear Him from generation to generation. He hath shown strength with His arm; He hath scattered the proud in the imagination of their hearts. He hath put down the mighty from their seats, and exalted them of low degree. He hath filled the hungry with good things; and the rich He hath sent empty away. He hath helped His servant Israel, in remembrance of His mercy; as He spake to our fathers, to Abraham, and to His seed for ever."

—Luke 1:38, 46–55

Is it not interesting to note that God's most faithful and useful servants were those who said, "Yes, Lord," to whatever task He handed them? We see Mary, Paul, Esther, thousands of missionaries, and many others who are used by God in various, exciting ways. What is it about them? Why is their service so great? The key is their hearts. Their hearts are willing, willing to do whatever work God sets before them, whether it is great or small.

Wherever we may be, whatever we may be doing, let us always answer the Lord, as Mary did, honored to be His handmaid! It is such a joy to be able to say, "I am a servant of the Lord Jesus Christ!" Praise God for this opportunity and use it wisely for His glory!

Different Shapes, Different Sizes

"Nay but, O man, who art thou that repliest against God? Shall the thing formed say to him that formed it, Why hast thou made me thus? Hath not the potter power over the clay . . ." —Romans 9:20–21

When I watched the professional potter make things out of clay, he had sample projects all around his station. There were jars, pots, bowls, pitchers, cups, and various items. Some were very large; others were rather small. Still, each was unique and special in its own way. Each piece had a different purpose.

Service that the Lord has for us comes in different shapes and different sizes! ☺ It is a sad thing when people overlook some of the tasks that God assigns His people. For example, the fulfillment in being a wife and mother is highly overlooked and often thought of as one of the least important jobs a woman can have.

There have been times in my life when I have overlooked the importance of a job I was given. I remember when I was younger, my father and brother Justin were working steadily at building a deck for our above-the-ground pool. I could easily watch their labor from our bay window in the kitchen and would look out wistfully, wondering why I could not go help. Why was I here just helping around the house? Surely that did not do much toward the production of the deck!

However, when the boys got hungry and needed a meal, my mother and I were preparing it. I began to see the importance of my duty. Without our work, the boys would be unable to complete theirs.

When I think of someone who has demonstrated service by accepting any job she receives, mothers are one of the first to come to mind. Secondly, I recall a home schooling seminar that had classes for parents, teens, and children. My parents gave Justin and me permission to work as teachers in the children's workshop. A dear friend of mine, however, had lovingly and selflessly taken the duty of staying home with her younger siblings so that her parents could attend the parents' workshops. She had a very cheerful attitude about the task she was to take on, and she set a good example for me of a true servant.

The jobs and tasks that God gives you come in different shapes and sizes. Do not be jealous if your friend is on a mission trip to India while you are at home helping your mother with the household. God will bless you for your willingness to serve Him in whatever ways He sees fit.

An Humble Servant

When I think of a humble servant, I often think of my mother. She does large amounts of "background" work for the *Virtuous Daughters* ministry. When I type the monthly magazine, she is the overall editor who makes suggestions and "polishes" it. She helps with a lot of the work that I do not enjoy, like folding and stapling, putting on stamps, taking it to the copy store, etc. Her work for the magazine is vital, yet others can easily overlook it. What an humble servant my mother is! Thank you, Mommy, for your service! ♥

Our greatest example of a true servant is Jesus Christ Himself. He showed humility and selflessness to all those around Him. We are to follow His lead. *"But he that is greatest among you shall be your servant. And whosoever shall exalt himself shall be abased; and he that shall humble himself shall be exalted."*—Matthew 23:11–12

"If there be therefore any consolation in Christ, if any comfort of love, if any fellowship of the Spirit, if any bowels and mercies, fulfill ye my joy, that ye be likeminded, having the same love, being of one accord, of one mind. Let nothing be done through strife or vainglory; but in lowliness of mind let each esteem other better than themselves. Look not every man on his own things, but every man also on the things of others. Let this mind be in you, which was also in Christ Jesus: Who, being in the form of God, thought it not robbery to be equal with God: but made Himself of no reputation, and took upon Him the form of a servant, and was made in the likeness of men: and being found in fashion as a man, He humbled Himself, and became obedient unto death, even the death of the cross. Wherefore God also hath highly exalted Him, and given Him a name which is above every name: that at the name of Jesus every knee should bow, of things in heaven, and things in earth, and things under the earth; And that every tongue should confess that Jesus Christ is Lord, to the glory of God the Father. Wherefore, my beloved, as ye have always obeyed, not as in my presence only, but now much more in my absence, work out your own salvation with fear and trembling. For it is God which worketh in you both to will and to do of His good pleasure. Do all things without murmurings and disputings: that ye may be blameless and harmless, the sons of God, without rebuke, in the midst of a

> crooked and perverse nation, among whom ye shine as lights in the world; holding forth the word of life; that I may rejoice in the day of Christ, that I have not run in vain, neither laboured in vain. Yea, and if I be offered upon the sacrifice and service of your faith, I joy, and rejoice with you all."
>
> *—Philippians 2:1–17*

Without Christ . . .

> *"I am the vine, ye are the branches: He that abideth in Me, and I in him, the same bringeth forth much fruit: for without Me ye can do nothing."*
>
> *—John 15:5*

The lump of clay sitting on the table is nothing until the potter does something with it. Without the potter, the clay is *nothing*. So are we without Christ—nothing. On the contrary, we can do great things for God if we allow Him to work through us.

As I neared the end of seventh grade, I was discouraged and concerned about the number of upcoming tests. All the studying I needed to do in a matter of days overwhelmed me. My attitude was one of self-pity even though I was trying to have a happy heart.

God used *Philippians 4:13:* "I can do all things through Christ which strengtheneth me." to draw me closer to Him that month. I realized that it was only through Christ that I could be joyful and strong.

You might feel this way as well. You want to serve the Lord, and you are trying to, but something is not clicking. Something is going wrong. You try and try, yet you fail. What is the problem? You might consider the fact that you are nothing and can do nothing good in yourself. It is only through Christ.

Ask the Lord for forgiveness and start fresh. Ask Him to work through you from here out and be His vessel to flow through. Whenever I am struggling to serve the Lord, I must examine the situation— am I trying to serve Him and do good things in my own strength? If so, that is the problem, because *". . . without Me ye can do nothing."—John 15:5* and *"For with God nothing shall be impossible."—Luke 1:37* I appreciate the following quote, possibly founded on these Scriptures:

"Without the assistance of the Divine Being . . . I cannot succeed. With that assistance, I cannot fail."

—Abraham Lincoln

Let me encourage you to allow God to work through you! Trying to do things in your own strength will discourage you quickly. *"The joy of the LORD is your strength."*—Nehemiah 8:10

To Whom Much is Given . . .

". . . For unto whomsoever much is given, of him shall be much required: and to whom men have committed much, of him they will ask the more."

—Luke 12:48

God has blessed us with so much—and we appreciate it. I thank God for my grandmother who has taught me so much about computers. However, with this blessing comes the responsibilities and requirements. When someone in my family has a problem or question about their work on the computer, I am usually the first person they ask. And if *I* cannot help, we call my grandmother! ☺ God has gifted each of us. Sometimes we think that the nicest way to use those gifts is to keep them to ourselves. The Bible says, however, that we should use and multiply our talents—not bury them!

I think sometimes we fail to realize that with *blessings* comes *responsibility*. This is true with everyone. We have noticed that living on five wooded acres brings the joys of frequent hospitality! ☺ Having a boat and wave runners means keeping them running, which is sometimes a big job!

We need to take into account that when God blesses us, He expects us to use those blessings to bless others. Cheerfully and frequently, we should give what we can to others. Whatever God has blessed you with, you will also be required to give and serve.

Minute's Notice!

"My heart is ever at your service."—Shakespeare

Shortly before the War for Independence in the 1700s, there was a group of colonists with the nickname "minutemen," because they were ready to do whatever they were ordered to in a minute's notice! Regardless of the weather, the time of the day, or the location they were, these men were prepared. Does this describe our attitude of serving? Are we ready to serve someone if we receive orders from the Lord "out of the blue"?

"Let your loins be girded about, and your lights burning; and ye yourselves like unto men that wait for their lord, when he will return from the wedding; that when he cometh and knocketh, they may open unto him immediately. Blessed are those servants, whom the lord when he cometh shall find watching: verily I say unto you, that he shall gird himself, and make them to sit down to meat, and will come forth and serve them. And if he shall come in the second watch, or come in the third watch, and find them so, blessed are those servants. And this know, that if the goodman of the house had known what hour the thief would come, he would have watched, and not have suffered his house to be broken through. Be ye therefore ready also: for the Son of man cometh at an hour when ye think not."
—Luke 12:35–40

Some people can be very well described as "ready in a minute's notice." They are "quick on their feet" when something happens unexpectedly. Other people, like myself, are slower at reacting to things that happen. I have tried to improve! ☺

Recently, I volunteered to help with a spelling bee. To my dismay, the coordinator has not informed me how I will be helping! ☹ This could mean one of several things: I may not be helping at all, she may have me registering children, I may sit in front of all the parents, siblings, and guests to be a "scribe," or I could be responsible for making sure the children are all in the correct seats, or it could be—who knows what?!

I really want to know ahead of time, but it looks like I will not. Therefore, I have concluded that when I get there, I will simply ask the coordinator what I can do to help, be sure I understand my instructions, and then get to work. I need to be ready to do whatever she needs me to at a minute's notice.

Who are some examples in the Bible of people whom God suddenly gave instruction to do something? God chose them for a work because they had willing hearts that could be easily molded. Mary, Paul, Esther, and the Good Samaritan were all willing and ready when God called them.

Another area I would like to encourage you in "a minute's notice" is taking initiative to serve in different ways. We know a family with eight lovely daughters. Each time they come over, the first thing the girls ask is how they can help. It is such a blessing, and they are prepared for whatever task we assign them!

As Unto the Lord

"And whatsoever ye do in word or deed, do all in the name of the Lord Jesus, giving thanks to God and the Father by Him. Servants, obey in all things your masters according to the flesh; not with eyeservice, as menpleasers; but in singleness of heart, fearing God: and whatsoever ye do, do it heartily, as to the Lord, and not unto men; knowing that of the Lord ye shall receive the reward of the inheritance: for ye serve the Lord Christ." —Colossians 3:17, 22–24

How many times do we do a service, and say it is for the Lord, but we fail to prove that by an unhappy attitude, a sloppy job, or a slothful pace. This is not doing something as unto the Lord. If President Bush were to come over to our house for dinner, I think I would set the table very neatly and with a cheerful heart! ☺ The sad thing, however, is that Jesus Christ does not get that same cheerfulness from me every night. This principle of "as unto the Lord" is very important for every girl to learn.

Why do we do things only unto people? People are fickle—people change. I remember a neighbor who lived down the street and came over often. We had just had a new baby, and if he was fussing when she got here, she would say, "You need to get that baby up; you shouldn't let him cry like that!" Next time she came over and the baby was fussing, I was quick to get him up, because I wanted to please this person. When I walked into the living room with him, she said, "You are spoiling that baby! Why do you always get him out of bed just because he's crying a little?"

I smiled, but inside I was thinking, *Well, which way do you want it?* ☺ Now I realize the error of my way; I was striving to please a person. When I do that, I have to constantly change the way I live my life because every person has a different suggestion, different idea of the way I should live it. God, on the other hand, has one idea, one way for me to live my life. If I am striving to please *Him*, then I can have one main and wholesome focus. *"Jesus Christ the same yesterday, and today, and for ever."*—Hebrews 13:8

Are you only striving to please people in your service? The table needs to be cleaned according to your mother's standards, and your service to an elderly couple's yard needs to be done as they asked, but do your work as unto the Lord. Do it just as they ask and with a cheerful heart! Is that not how we would do it for our Lord?

> *"Servants, be obedient to them that are your masters according to the flesh, with fear and trembling, in singleness of your heart, as unto Christ; not with eyeservice, as menpleasers; but as the servants of Christ, doing the will of God from the heart; with good will doing service, as to the Lord, and not to men: knowing that whatsoever good thing any man doeth, the same shall he receive of the Lord, whether he be bond or free."* —Ephesians 6:5–8

Is the service that you do unto the Lord, and from your heart? Mr. Bill Gothard tells a story from when he was a child. He and his brother shared a bedroom. While Mr. Gothard was organized and liked his things picked up, his brother was the opposite. Mr. Gothard said that each morning he would make his bed and make his brother's too, just hoping to get his brother to appreciate it and start making it on his own.

His brother appreciated Mr. Gothard's service, but it really made no difference to him whether his bed was made or not. (Sound familiar with one of your siblings? ☺) Mr. Gothard was quickly discouraged by the work he was doing—and nothing seemed to change in his brother's daily habits. He later realized that he was doing this work to his brother, and not the Lord. When he began making the bed *for the Lord* his attitude changed, and he could make it without frustration. ☺

The children's conference that I referred to earlier was very stressful. We had around twenty-five kids ages four to twelve in a little area half the size of my bedroom! Puny stations just like ours were set up all around the large auditorium. It was loud, many of the children could not hear what I was trying to teach them, and I was confused. All they had to do to get away was cross the tapeline, and I did not want to be missing any children!

The whole day Justin and I talked over the noise and tried to teach them from God's Word, but we felt that there was no effect. Later I realized that my heart was not right. Was I doing this unto the Lord Jesus or for the people who asked me to teach? Was I teaching this lesson because I longed to bring these children to Christ, or was I teaching it because that was what my agenda said to do that day? If I was not serving with my whole heart to please the Lord, it is no wonder the children were not getting it. Looking back, I realize it could have gone much better if we would have taught from our hearts and focused on allowing the *Lord* to work through us. As a result, the children would have been more responsive. (We did work on this the second day, and it went much better! ☺) *"For do I now persuade men, or God? or do I seek to please men? for if I yet pleased men, I should not be the servant of Christ."* —Galatians 1:10

Good and Faithful Servant

"Being then made free from sin, ye became the servants of righteousness. But now being made free from sin, and become servants to God, ye have your fruit unto holiness, and the end everlasting life."—Romans 6:18, 22

My father is always serving. His spiritual gift is service, and he has done a splendid job of actively using that gift to glorify God. He is constantly serving his family, neighbors, friends, and community. He served his country for three years in the U.S. Army, and he continues to serve his community as a Houston police officer. His service does not stop there, either! He is always serving his family. On long days of school or stressful days of running errands, my father will volunteer to make dinner or help with the chores. When a friend or neighbor needs help repairing his car, cutting down a tree, or fixing something, he is the first to be there. No one could ever repay my dad for the service he has done, but he has an eternal focus, and one day he will be praised, *". . . Well done, thou good and faithful servant: thou hast been faithful over a few things, I will make thee ruler over many things: enter thou into the joy of thy lord."—Matthew 25:21* Thank you, Daddy, for your excellent example of a good and faithful servant! ♥

My father's example challenges me—do we all serve in this manner? Is it a never-ending service to the Lord and others? Do you tire of serving, or do you joy in it? It is not in vain! *"Therefore, my beloved brethren, be ye steadfast, unmoveable, always abounding in the work of the Lord, forasmuch as ye know that your labour is not in vain in the Lord."—1 Corinthians 15:58*

Strive to be a diligent, active servant who is always doing something to the good of someone else. I must work on this, especially in my own home. Nevertheless, God rewards those who are faithful in even the little areas—helping with dinner, feeding spaghetti to a hungry two-year-old, getting a cup of water for a too-short toddler, and earnestly serving your father and mother. In fact, if you can be a servant in these things, you will likely be able to be a servant in any way God calls you. He will reward you for serving Him from your heart with a happy spirit. *"He that is faithful in that which is least is faithful also in much . . ."—Luke 16:10*

Application...

"But be ye doers of the word, and not hearers only, deceiving your own selves." James 1:22

Do you have a willing heart that you allow God to mold to His image? _____

Would others label you as a servant? _____ In what ways do you serve others? _____

How do you serve in your own family? _____

List two Scriptures about being a servant: _____

Choose one of the following verses to memorize and recite:

Matthew 25:21   *Matthew 23:11–12*
Ephesians 6:5–8   *Luke 1:38, 46–55*
Philippians 2:1–17 *Isaiah 64:8*

Recited to: _____ Date: _____

Choose one of the following activities to work on:

- If you do not have assigned chores, ask your parents to give you some, and be responsible for them each day.

- Write an essay on the joy of serving.

- Find a way to serve those outside of your home too, if your parents feel that would be beneficial to you.

"*I had utterly abandoned* myself to Him . . . Could any choice be as wonderful as His will? Did not He assure me by His very presence that His thoughts toward us are good, and not evil? Death to my own plans and desires was almost deliriously delightful. Everything was laid at His nail-scarred feet, life or death, health or illness, appreciation by others, or misunderstanding, success or failure as measured by human standards. Only He Himself mattered."

—V. Raymond Edman, missionary to Ecuador

"Give her of the fruit of her hands; and let her own works praise her in the gates."—Proverbs 31:31

Dear Sister,
 Isn't a relationship with Jesus Christ exciting? Don't you just long to know Him better and strive to serve Him with a more willing heart? Do not hesitate; start today!
 Of course you will have struggles; there will no doubt be trials along the way. But never forget Who you are walking with, Who is upholding you every step. You cannot see what the future holds, but you will forever know Who holds it. Trust in His goodness and His will for your life. Cling to your Lord, the Author and Finisher of your faith! He is so good to those who love Him!
 Never forget that the girl you are today decides the woman you will be tomorrow. Allow the Lord to work through you to conform you to His image. Let us all be praying to become virtuous daughters of noble character.
  Because He Lives,
   Tiffany

> "WHEREFORE SEEING we also are compassed about with so great a cloud of witnesses, let us lay aside every weight, and the sin which doth so easily beset us, and lets us run with patience the race that is set before us, looking unto Jesus the author and finisher of our faith: Who for the joy that was set before Him endured the cross, despising the shame, and is set down at the right hand of the throne of God. For consider Him that endured such contradiction of sinners against Himself, lest ye be wearied and faint in your minds." —Hebrews 12:1–3

Challenge to American Women ... by Peter Marshall

"The modern challenge to motherhood is the eternal challenge—that of being godly women. The very phrase sounds strange in our ears. We never hear it now.

"We hear about every other kind of woman—beautiful women, smart women, sophisticated women, career women, talented women, divorced women.

"But so seldom do we hear of a godly woman—or of a godly man either, for that matter. I believe women come nearer fulfilling their God-given function in the home than anywhere else.

"It is a much nobler thing to be a good wife than to be Miss America.

"It is a greater achievement to establish a Christian home than it is to produce a second-rate novel, filled with filth.

"It is a far, far better thing in the realms of morals to be old-fashioned than to be ultra-modern.

"The world has enough women who know how to hold their cocktails, who have lost all their illusions and their faith.

"The world has enough women who know how to be smart. It needs women who are willing to be simple.

"The world has enough women who know how to be brilliant. It needs some who will be brave.

"The world has enough women who are popular. It needs more who are pure.

"We need women, and men, too, who would rather be morally right than socially correct.

"Let us not fool ourselves—without Christianity, without Christian education, without the principles of Christ inculcated into young life, we are simply rearing pagans.

"Physically, they will be perfect. Intellectually, they will be brilliant. But spiritually, they will be pagan. Let us not fool ourselves.

"The twentieth century challenge to motherhood—when it is all boiled down—is that mothers will have an experience of God . . . a reality which they can pass on to their children."

Taken from Elizabeth Beall Phillips's book, <u>Verses of Virtue</u>. Available from Vision Forum Ministries; see "Godly Resources."

Godly Resources...

The following companies sell books and/or cassette tapes (or CDs) that are wholesome and edifying. Most of the items I recommended can be purchased from one of the following:

Vision Forum
1-800-440-0022
www.visionforum.com

Keepers of the Faith
906-663-6881
www.keepersofthefaith.com

Mantle Ministries
228 Still Ridge
Bulverde, TX 78613
www.mantlemin.com

Castleberry Farms Press
P.O. Box 337
Poplar, WI 54864

Other:

His Chosen Bride, by Jennifer J. Lamp
Available from: Grace Works, 1421 Lieunette, Wichita, KS 67203

"Godly Daughter Checklist"; "Sarah's Beauty Secret," both by Renee Ellison
Available from: Crossover.Ellison.net or
Cross Over, FLC 7028, Durango, CO 81301

Bibliography

Though attempts were made to receive written permission for each source quoted, there were a few exceptions where no response was received. In these cases, we trust that the publisher and/or author is willing to allow the quoting of brief passages. Thank you.

Chapter One
1. Wychopen, Forrest, *Abide in Christ*. (Xulon Press: USA 2003), 77–78, 88
2. Auge, Brianna, "Cooking" *Virtuous Daughters* (July 2003), 7
3. Mueller, George, *The Autobiography of George Muller*. (Whitaker House: New Kensington, PA 1984), 47–48
4. Lamp, Jennifer, *His Chosen Bride*. (GraceWorks Ministry Press: Wichita, KS 1999), 25–26
5. Wychopen, Forrest, *Abide in Christ*. (Xulon Press: USA 2003), 89–90

Chapter Two
1. J. H. St. A, *The Basket of Flowers*. (SAT Publications: 1996), 48–49
2. Mueller, George, *The Autobiography of George Muller*. (Whitaker House: New Kensington, PA 1984), 158
3. Riddell, Tara, "To God be the Glory" *Virtuous Daughters* (March 2005), 6
4. The Gideons International. (The Gideons International: Nashville, TN)
5. Newcomb, Harvey, *How To Be A Lady*. (1850; reprint, Crown Rights Book Company: Dahlonega, Georgia 2005), 62–63
6. Schlichter, Cheryl, "Prayer" *Virtuous Daughters* (September 2001), 3

Chapter Three
1. Prentiss, Elizabeth, *Stepping Heavenward*. (Barbour Publishing, Inc.: Uhrichsville, Ohio 1998), 303–304
2. Miller, J.R, *Home-Making*. (1882; reprint Vision Forum: San Antonio, TX 2003,) pp. 67–68
3. Mally, Sarah, Stephen, and Grace, *Making Brothers and Sisters Best Friends*. (Tomorrow's Forefathers: Cedar Rapids, IA 2002), 39

Chapter Four
1. Goforth, Noelle Wheeler, editor, *Daughters of Destiny*. (Mantle Ministries: Bulverde, TX 2000), 13
2. Phillips, Elizabeth Beall, editor, *Verses of Virtue*. (Vision Forum: San Antonio,

TX 2003), 58–59
3. Newcomb, Harvey, *How To Be A Lady*. (1850; reprint, Crown Rights Book Company: Dahlonega, GA 2005), 24
4. Ellison, Renee, *Sarah's Beauty Secret*. (2001), 4
5. Newcomb, Harvey, *How To Be A Lady*. (1850; reprint, Crown Rights Book Company: Dahlonega, Georgia 2005), 27–28
6. Ibid., 35–36
7. Schlichter, Cheryl L, "The Best Gift You Can Ever Give Your Parents" *Virtuous Daughters* (December 2004), 3–5

Chapter Five
1. Newcomb, Harvey, *How To Be A Lady*. (1850; reprint, Crown Rights Book Company: Dahlonega, Georgia 2005), 39
2. Mally, Sarah, Stephen, and Grace, *Making Brothers and Sisters Best Friends*. (Tomorrow's Forefathers: Cedar Rapids, IA 2002), 210
3. Miller, J. R, *Home-Making*. (1882; reprint Vision Forum: San Antonio, TX 2003), 156
4. Goforth, Noelle Wheeler, editor, *Daughters of Destiny*. (Mantle Ministries: Bulverde, TX 2000), 13

Chapter Six
1. Landis, Mary M, *Dear Princess*. (Rod and Staff Publishers: Crockett, Kentucky 1973), 198
2. Hulin, Sarah, "Letter Writing Fun" *Virtuous Daughters* (December 2002), 3

Chapter Seven
1. Wilder, Laura Ingalls, *By the Shores of Silver Lake*. (1939; reprint HarperCollins Publishers: New York, NY 1971), 95–96
2. Ellison, Renee, *Godly Daughter Checklist*. (1996), 3
3. Howard, Mildred T, *These Are My People*. (Bob Jones University Press: Greensville, SC 1984), 63
4. Phillips, Elizabeth Beall, *Verses of Virtue*. (Vision Forum: San Antonio, TX 2003), 93
5. Zakula, Susan D, *The Joy of Womanhood*. (Keepers of the Faith: Ironwood, MI 1993), 11
6. Newcomb, Harvey, *How To Be A Lady*. (1850; reprint, Crown Rights Book Company: Dahlonega, Georgia 2005), 48
7. Child, Mrs. L. Maria, *The Girl's Own Book*. (Applewood Books: Bedford, MA 1834), 281–283

Chapter Eight
1. Landis, Mary M, *Dear Princess*. (Rod and Staff Publishers, Inc: Crockett, Kentucky 1973), 227

Chapter Nine

1. Goforth, Noelle Wheeler, editor, *Daughters of Destiny* (Mantle Ministries: Bulverde, TX 2000), 11–12
2. Ewing, Donna, "Proverbs 31 Study" *Virtuous Daughters* (December 2002), 5–6
3. Child, Mrs. L. Maria, *The Girl's Own Book*. (Applewood Books: Bedford, MA 1834), 284
4. Phillips, Elizabeth Beall, editor, *Verses of Virtue* (Vision Forum: San Antonio, TX 2003), 109
5. Hulin, Sarah, "The Art of Letter Writing" *Virtuous Daughters* (July 2004), 4

Chapter Eleven

1. Norris, Kathleen, *Mother*. (1912; Restored and revised version; Vision Forum: San Antonio, TX 2002), 181–183
2. Schlichter, Cheryl L, "Proverbs 31 Study" *Virtuous Daughters* (September 2002), 5
3. Zakula, Susan D, *The Joy of Womanhood*. (Keepers of the Faith: Ironwood, MI 1993), 15
4. Seymour, John, *The Forgotten Arts and Crafts*. (Dorling Kindersley Publishing, Inc.: New York, NY 2001), 194
5. Zakula, Susan D, *The Joy of Womanhood*. (Keepers of the Faith: Ironwood, MI 1993), 21
6. Grady, Henry Woodfin, "If I Live Till Sundown." (public domain)
7. J. H. St. A, *The Basket of Flowers*. (SAT Publishers: 1996), 75

Some short quotes and poems have not been listed.

With Gratitude

I extend sincere appreciation to—

My dear father—your support and encouragement to never give up. Without it, I would not be where I am today. Also, your gracious help checking verses.

�

My dear mother—your time and effort to edit this book again and again, as well as constant assistance with the whole project. Also, your continual prayers and encouragement. It would have never been completed without you.

�

My dear brother Justin—your kind sense of humor throughout the project, as well as the time you sacrificed to help me check the Scriptures!

�

My dear sister Brittany—for taking some of my responsibilities so I could work on this book. Also for the many hours you spent helping me check Scriptures. What would I do without your cheerful help?!

�

My dear brothers, Gideon and Ethan, and the Twins on the way— I love you all so much, and thank God for your smiles!

�

My dear grandmother, Nanny—your encouragement and financial support. Thank you for being so generous.

�

Kristin Youngblood and Hannah Hulin—your thorough critique of this book. I was so impressed with your dedication and selflessness! It means a lot.

�

Laura Shaffer—your hours of editing and willingness to teach me many important techniques along the way. The book would not have come out right without your polishing!

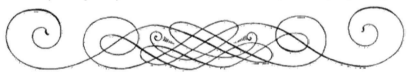

Jesus Christ, my Lord and Savior—
Thanks be to God for His unspeakable gift!

Also available through Virtuous Daughters Publications

Encouragement to the Home School Student by Tiffany Schlichter. This 85-page book is written to encourage young home school students to press on in their work, to be grateful to and honor their parents, to be diligent, to grow in the Lord, and more. The many Bible verses shared give the book a Scriptural base, and your child is sure to enjoy the humor along with the stories included! Written by a twelve-year-old home school student herself, the author is sure to share the weaknesses and struggles in her own life as well as beneficial ways to break these bad habits! (Limited supply.)

Recommended ages: 6–12   Price: $5.00+ shipping

Noble Girlhood: Becoming a Daughter of Victory and Virtue by Tiffany Schlichter. This 229-page paperback is addressed to young ladies. Tiffany comes as a friend to encourage girls in being virtuous daughters and living noble lives. Topics include: wise speech, honoring parents, loving siblings, wise friendships, finding victory in Jesus, service, purity, beauty, and many more! As always, Tiffany's book is packed with Scriptures.

Recommended ages: 10+   Price: 14.00+ shipping

Frisky all Year by Brittany Schlichter. This fun-filled fiction is sure to excite any young reader! It is an adventurous story about a young girl named Rachel and her pony Frisky. Children will learn the values of strong family-friendships, as well as the joys of working together.

Recommended ages: 4–10

Price: $1.00+ shipping

<u>**Make checks payable to Tiffany Schlichter.**</u>

Order Form

Please feel free to copy this form for your order.

Mail form and payment to:
Tiffany Schlichter
P.O. Box 98
Willis, TX 77378

Noble Girlhood: Becoming a Daughter of Victory and Virtue
$14.00 each

Quantity:_____ ---------------------------Subtotal: _____

Shipping: $2.00 first book, $1.00 per additional book------ _____

Encouragement to the Home School Student **$5.00 each**

Quantity:_____ --------------------------- Subtotal: _____

Shipping: $1.50 first book, $1.00 per additional book------ _____

Frisky all Year **$1.00 each**

Quantity:_____ ------------------ ---------Subtotal: _____

Shipping: $.50 per book -------------------------------- _____

TOTAL for ALL books: _____

SHIP TO:
NAME_____
ADDRESS_____
CITY_____STATE_____ZIP_____
PHONE _____

Mail-In Form

Did you complete this book? If so, I am offering you a small gift of appreciation if you also complete this form and mail it to me.

What was your favorite chapter? _____

Why? _____
_____

What did God teach you through the book? _____
_____
_____

What in particular did you like about this book? _____
_____
_____

What would you change about this book? _____
_____
_____

How did you find out about it? _____
_____

Anything else? (comments, questions) _____
_____
_____
_____
_____
_____

-Notes-

About the Author—

At the time of this writing, Tiffany M. Schlichter is sixteen years old and completing the tenth grade. She lives in Montgomery, Texas, on five acres with her parents and four younger siblings. Other than writing and encouraging fellow sisters in the Lord, Tiffany enjoys sewing, reading, corresponding with pen pals, spending time with her family, and the outdoors. She publishes *Virtuous Daughters*, a small monthly magazine for girls, and hopes to write more books in the future.

She would love to hear from any of her readers! Please write to her at:
Tiffany Schlichter
P.O. Box 98
Willis, TX 77378

"*Finally, brethren, whatsoever things are true, whatsoever things are honest, whatsoever things are just, whatsoever things are pure, whatsoever things are lovely, whatsoever things are of good report; if there be any virtue, and if there be any praise, think on these things.*"
—Philippians 4:8

Photo taken by Justin T. Schlichter

The Story Behind this Book...

I was about ten or eleven years old as I discussed "publishing" a book with Daddy. He was vacuuming out our swimming pool, but his task did nothing to keep him from talking. As I stood there pondering his knowledge and words of wisdom, I began to dream of an elaborate book which I could get published with the name *Tiffany M. Schlichter* printed on the cover.

My parents did much to encourage me in my dreams, and at thirteen years old I had finished writing my first book, *Encouragement to the Home School Student*. After much prayer, a generous contribution from my dear parents, and my selfless mother's enduring critiquing and editing skills, I published that book at the age of fourteen. Several bookstores carried it, and I was excited about the many doors God opened because of it.

Every penny I made from *Encouragement to the Home School Student* I stored in a savings account. My goal was to have enough money to publish my next book, whatever it might be. Praise the Lord, the book you are holding in your hands was published with saved-up money, as well as a generous contribution from a dear family member.

I give all praise and glory to the Lord Jesus Christ! And I also appreciate my dear parents' constant efforts and prayers through all my writing projects! (Too many to count! ☺) I hope that the Lord is able to use anything I have written to draw the readers closer to Him and His Word.

Because He Lives,
    Tiffany M. Schlichter